SPY SATELLITES

AND OTHER INTELLIGENCE TECHNOLOGIES

THAT CHANGED HISTORY

THOMAS GRAHAM JR. AND **KEITH A. HANSEN**

UNIVERSITY OF WASHINGTON PRESS Seattle and London

SPY

SATELLITES

and Other
Intelligence
Technologies
That Changed
History

This publication was supported in part by the Donald R. Ellegood International Publications Endowment.

University of Washington Press
P.O. Box 50096, Seattle, WA 98145 U.S.A.
www.washington.edu/uwpress

All statements of fact, opinion, or analysis expressed are those of the authors and do not reflect official positions or views of any U.S. government agency or department. Nothing in the contents of this book should be construed as asserting or implying U.S. government authentication of information or endorsement of the authors' views. This material has been reviewed to prevent the disclosure of classified information.

Library of Congress Cataloging-in-Publication Data
can be found at the back of the book

The paper used in this publication is acid-free and 90 percent recycled from at least 50 percent post-consumer waste. It meets the minimum requirements of American National Standard for Information Sciences—Permanence of Paper for Printed Library Materials, ANSI Z39.48-1984.

TO THOSE who have devoted their expertise and energies to providing the best information possible to support U.S. national security deliberations and arms control initiatives. In particular, to the memory of our colleague and friend, Howard Stoertz, for selfless dedication to his country, leadership within the U.S. Intelligence Community, and a unique contribution to efforts to defuse the nuclear arms race.

Contents

APPENDIXES

Foreword

TOM GRAHAM AND KEITH HANSEN—both experts, one on legal and

policy issues and the other on verification issues—collaborated on

several arms control negotiations as members of U.S. delegations.

This book is based on their long and personal experience in the arms

control arena. As professionals, they give us a helpful and accurate

overview of the interplay between diplomacy, intelligence capabili-

ties, and international arms control policies, a major component of

U.S. foreign policy during the Cold War. And the story they tell is a success story of intelligence and verification capabilities that made arms control possible.

National Technical Means (NTM) is an arms control code word connoting an array of satellite, airborne, and ground- or sea-based sensors and associated analytical methodologies used by the U.S. Intelligence Community to observe and assess foreign military weapons and force developments. As a generic term, NTM was used for purposes of negotiations and in treaty texts without actually disclosing, and thus compromising, intelligence sources or methods. NTM capabilities are used to monitor and to verify arms control treaties. To monitor a treaty is to observe and report activities surrounding controlled (i.e., limited or banned) capabilities. Verification is a legal and policy determination that the observed activities are either permitted or are violations of a treaty's terms. The Intelligence Community monitors agreements. The Department of State and the National Security Council verify the treaties.

Early in the 1950s, as the Cold War became increasingly characterized by a strategic nuclear arms competition, the effectiveness of Soviet security rendered traditional intelligence collection methods inadequate. In the absence of data, debates over the "bomber gap" and the "missile gap" erupted in the United States and spilled over into presidential politics. At the direction of President Eisenhower, the Intelligence Community, in conjunction with industry, moved to create a remote sensing capability that could gather information on Soviet strategic forces. Major programs were launched in overhead imagery collection—the U-2 aircraft and Corona satellite—and in the collection of signals intelligence from ground-, air-, sea-, and space-based sensors. Their initial purpose was to answer policy questions and to support defense planning. But by the early 1970s, this array of intelligence programs had matured to a level of sophistication that it could promise the two qualities upon which the verification of arms control agreements could rest: independence and reliability. That is, without the USSR's permission or cooperation, the United States could assess Soviet strategic force developments independently; and, the data from such assessments were sufficient in quantity and quality to be accurate and, therefore, reliable.

This book focuses primarily on the Intelligence Community's contribution to harnessing the nuclear arms race through monitoring the development and eventual control of intercontinental ballistic missiles, submarine-launched ballistic missiles, and intercontinental-range bombers, which were the primary public measure of a superpower's relative status. The arms control process that is described, however, and its support by the Intelligence Community is similar to negotiations on other types of military forces such as the Anti-Ballistic Missile Treaty, the Intermediate-Range Nuclear Forces Treaty, and the Treaty on Conventional Armed Forces in Europe (theater forces) negotiations that unfolded during the Cold War.

This book will be appreciated, I believe, by students of the arms control process as part of the larger record on Cold War relations between the superpowers. In conjunction with other books in the field, such as the *Wizards of Langley*, *Deep Black*, and other chronicles of technical collection, along with accounts of the various negotiations, this story gives an expanded appreciation of what was done with the information gleaned from the Intelligence Community's technical collection and analysis to support major policy and diplomatic undertakings. It describes some of the middle ground (necessarily in sketchy detail) between why certain technical systems were created and how the output was used. Moreover, in one passage, the authors point out that one reason for secrecy in the satellite reconnaissance program was to prevent the international legal strictures barring unauthorized aircraft overflights from being extended to space surveillance. This is a little-known fact among professional intelligence officers and the first reference to it that I have seen in print. The strategy was successful, and this may help a reader appreciate why official silence on satellite reconnaissance was maintained long after it was an open secret in the press.

Other literature will have to be consulted for understanding the economic, political, and strategic imperatives that led both super-powers to the bargaining table. But the fact that agreements limiting, reducing, and banning strategic nuclear forces were negotiated and ratified at the height of the Cold War is a tribute to the ability of the negotiators to craft it and to the Intelligence Community to ensure that the limitations could be monitored and, therefore, effectively verified. From the perspective of one who spent many years analyzing Soviet military forces, I can say with confidence that Tom Graham and Keith Hansen are to be commended for their roles in the various negotiations and for the excellent presentation of the story they tell in this book.

ROBERT M. HUFFSTUTLER

EXECUTIVE DIRECTOR (RET.)

CENTRAL INTELLIGENCE AGENCY

Preface and **Acknowledgments**

INTELLIGENCE—what it is and what it has contributed to U.S.

national security—is often misunderstood and misrepresented.

Unfortunately, the secrecy that necessarily surrounds national intel-

ligence tends to perpetuate a general level of ignorance and allows

free rein to those who wish to mischaracterize it in the media. For-

tunately, a few authors have been able to rise above the din of mis-

information and present a more correct, if not complete, picture of what intelligence is and how it functions. One of the best general explanations of intelligence is available in Mark Lowenthal's *Intelligence: From Secrets to Policy*. In this present volume, we want to help clarify some of the mystique, but we also wish to provide an as-yet-unrecorded account of how U.S. intelligence capabilities contributed to the end of the Cold War by facilitating the negotiation of strategic nuclear arms control agreements.

Intelligence has made a unique but largely unheralded contribution to world peace with respect to arms control. Over a thirty-year period, improved intelligence capabilities eliminated the time-honored practice of worst-casing the strategic capabilities of the Soviet Union, which had made the early Cold War years exceedingly dangerous. The United States and its allies and partners attempted, in part through arms control initiatives, to reduce the risk of war involving nuclear weapons or other weapons of mass destruction (WMD) and to increase world stability. Modern intelligence capabilities deserve much of the credit for making such achievements possible.

We wish to shed light on the critical role that "national technical means" (NTM) of verification, a euphemism for remote technical intelligence collection capabilities and intelligence analysis, played in the significant accomplishments of the past four decades in increasing U.S. and world security by harnessing the nuclear arms race and preventing, at least to some degree, efforts to proliferate nuclear and other WMD. While there remains much to be done in this arena, intelligence—both collection and analysis, aided by the expertise and partnership of U.S. industry—has done much to make these accomplishments possible.

But the U.S. Intelligence Community cannot rest on past achievements. For its capabilities to remain effective, national security tools, continued protection of sensitive sources and methods, and new advancements in technology and methodologies are needed. As was demonstrated by the Iraq WMD episode, the challenges of monitoring small, clandestine WMD programs in various parts of the world are vastly greater than those related to monitoring the large strategic nuclear forces that were of prime concern during the Cold War. Unfortunately, many of the details of advancements that have been made, or even of some current capabilities, must remain hidden from public view to ensure that they remain effective against the efforts of those who intend us harm. Nevertheless, there is an important story regarding past accomplishments that can and should be told. It is our hope that through this analysis the contributions to date of intelligence to these critical national security challenges will be understood and appreciated by those who value ongoing efforts to reduce nuclear arsenals and to prevent the proliferation of WMD, especially among international terrorists. To continue these important contributions to national security, current intelligence capabilities must be protected and further investments made to their advancement.

The opportunity to contribute to U.S. national security through service on arms control and nonproliferation delegations over the span of thirty years was one of the distinct privileges of our professional careers. We arrived on the scene with different backgrounds, but our paths continually crossed. Our teamwork and commitment to U.S. and international efforts to halt the nuclear arms race and to restrain the further proliferation of nuclear weapons was deeply satisfying. Although not all of the negotiating efforts were successful, attempts to negotiate and implement agreements have made the world a safer place, and we salute and thank those with whom we have served.

The decision to write this book was the result of a breakfast chat several years ago, when we were reflecting on what had helped make arms control agreements successful. Without reliable and effective verification, none of our efforts, especially in the bilateral U.S.-Soviet negotiations, would have been possible. Although books have been written about verification issues in general, little has been said about one key ingredient: U.S. national intelligence capabilities that facilitated the remote monitoring of Soviet strategic nuclear forces during the dark days of the Cold War. We agreed that we should record as much as possible about this aspect of verification to complete the record. Our objective has been to write an account that is informative to the general public, instructive to students of international relations, and helpful to those charged with formulating and executing future U.S. national security policy. We thank all who have contributed to its research, writing, and publication.

While this story focuses mainly on how U.S. policymakers capitalized on the novel intelligence capabilities that were developed during the Cold War, most of the credit for the development of sophisticated technical collection and analytic methodologies goes to dedicated experts in key agencies of the Intelligence Community who worked hand-in-glove with scientists and engineers from U.S. industry. None of the achievements about which we write would have happened without their hard work, creativity, and invaluable expertise.

We want to thank the following colleagues and experts for reviewing and critiquing the manuscript in an effort to make it as accurate, informative, and useful as possible. Sidney Drell, an expert on technical issues, has dedicated much of his career to improving U.S. monitoring and verification efforts; R. Evans Hineman, a technical intelligence expert, has worked tirelessly to help develop and effectively utilize U.S. national monitoring capabilities; and Robert M. Huffstutler, a senior intelligence manager and analyst, spent much of his career helping U.S. policymakers understand the military capabilities and intentions of the Soviet Union.

We are grateful also to Frances Eddy for her tireless efforts to ensure that the two of us stayed in synch as we worked on the manuscript from opposite sides of the continent. We thank Michael Duckworth and his associates at the University of Washington Press for their support during the publication process.

THOMAS GRAHAM JR.   **KEITH A. HANSEN**

SPY SATELLITES

AND OTHER INTELLIGENCE TECHNOLOGIES

THAT CHANGED HISTORY

Introduction

STALIN'S SOVIET RUSSIA, as the former Soviet Union was often called

during the early days of the Cold War, became a significant threat to

the United States and its allies in Western Europe and Asia at the

end of World War II. The Soviet Union represented not only a closed,

secretive society but also one that stretched from the Baltic and Black

seas to the Pacific Ocean and espoused an ideology-based global ambi-

tion for spreading Communist influence and control through brute military force and subversion. Thus, understanding what was transpiring within its vast expanse, particularly in terms of military force developments, became one of the biggest challenges of the Cold War. And after 1949, Communist China added significantly to the proportion of the earth's surface that was hidden behind the Iron and Bamboo curtains. The challenge of monitoring and understanding concealed military capabilities and intentions fell to Western intelligence services, especially those in the United States.

During the early days of the Cold War, efforts to understand Soviet, and subsequently Chinese, military capabilities, intentions, and national decision-making were compounded by the difficulty of following political and economic developments in those countries. Other countries such as Castro's Cuba, North Korea, North Vietnam, the Eastern European nations of the Warsaw Pact, post-1979 Iran, Libya, and Saddam Hussein's Iraq closed their borders over time and also became what are called hard targets for intelligence collection and analysis. This development added to the national security challenge facing the United States. Thus, growing U.S. policy and defense requirements dictated the need for ever more sophisticated and capable intelligence collection systems and corresponding analytical methodologies. The United States in particular devoted considerable resources to the development of new types of remote technical collection systems along with new analytic techniques in an effort to augment the reporting from clandestine human agent operations and liaison intelligence services.

After several decades of unconstrained competition and dangerously expanding strategic nuclear arsenals, both the USSR and the United States came to a point in their open-ended buildup of nuclear forces where they began to question how much military power was enough to ensure their security. However, early efforts to consider formal constraints on their growing military capabilities collapsed because of their mutual lack of trust and inability to provide credible independent verification of what the other side was saying or doing. Meaningful steps to halt the nuclear arms race became possible only when both sides finally possessed sufficiently capable and reliable remote technical intelligence collection systems, mainly in the form of photo and signals reconnaissance satellites. Consequently, not until the early 1970s did it become politically and practically feasible to negotiate and verify meaningful arms control measures, which contributed to the end of the Cold War.

In more recent decades, intelligence has often been the key to understanding the efforts of countries to clandestinely develop weapons of mass destruction (WMD) (chemical, biological, and/or nuclear weapons) and to proliferate WMD technology and knowledge around the globe. Despite the apparent overestimate of Iraq's chemical and biological weapon stockpiles prior to 2003, intelligence has more often than not been able sooner or later to discern the efforts and accomplishments of would-be proliferators such as North Korea, Iran, Libya, and the A.Q. Khan black market nuclear proliferation network.

Thus, intelligence collection and analysis have been and will continue to be an essential ingredient in U.S. and international efforts to limit, reduce, and eliminate nuclear arsenals as well as to deal with the threat posed by the proliferation of WMD. This, then, is the story of how the development and use of U.S. national technical intelligence capabilities contributed to the historic arms control achievements of the past forty years and to the end of the Cold War strategic rivalry between the United States and the Soviet Union.

1

To Verify or Not to Verify

ONE OF THE GREAT success stories of the Cold War was the development by the United States of intelligence sources and methods that were sufficiently effective to make it possible to understand the Soviet strategic threat more accurately, thus making worst-case military planning unnecessary. At last the United States could see into the interior of Soviet territory; limiting strategic arms became possible because for the first time the basic verification tools were available to both sides. To permit formal limitations on strategic nuclear weapons systems, the central deterrent systems of the Cold War, verification had to be effective and reliable. For the United States, there had to be a way to discern independently the military activities, capabilities, and, if possible, intentions of the Soviet Union, which as a closed society had nearly absolute control over all of its national security information.

What Is Verification?

In its most basic sense, verification is the ability of one side to ensure unilaterally and reliably that the military activities of the other party are not inconsistent with agreed treaty obligations and cannot put its national security at risk through cheating. In his testimony on the Intermediate-Range Nuclear Forces (INF) Treaty before the Senate Foreign Relations Committee on January 28, 1988, Ambassador Paul Nitze stated that the United States insists that any agreement must be effectively verifiable if it is to improve stability and make a lasting contribution to peace and security.[1] "Effectively verifiable," he said, meant if the other side moves beyond the limits of the treaty in any militarily significant way, we would be able to detect such a violation in time to respond and, thereby, deny the other side the benefit of the violation. He concluded by saying that the U.S. ability to detect and respond to violations helps to deter them in the first place.

Declarations vs. Verification

Limits on the activities related to some weapons systems are inherently unverifiable, such as biological weapons which can be made in a laboratory. In addition, there are some cases where independent verification of military activity is not essential because violations would not be strategically significant. Finally, there are cases where mere declarations rather than rigorous verification activities are all that is desired by the parties involved. Thus, several pre-1970 arms control treaties did not require verification because in those particular cases it was not possible, strategically essential, or politically necessary.

Therefore, it should be understood that verification of arms control agreements as we understand the concept today is generally a product of the nuclear arms race and the Cold War. Before the latter half of the twentieth century, verification was rarely an issue since most early efforts at arms control were declaratory, often taking the form of rules of warfare. Meaningful verification was simply either not relevant or feasible before a weapon system was used in combat. For example, the 1899 and 1907 Hague Peace declarations prohibited the use of poison gas weapons. When the German Army violated The Hague declarations on April 22, 1915, near Ypres, Belgium, by dispensing an estimated 150 tons of chlorine gas from thousands of cylinders, sophisticated verification systems were not necessary to detect this fact. More than five thousand Allied soldiers lay injured and dying from chlorine gas inhalation.[2] In a similar vein, the Geneva Protocol of 1925, which prohibited the use in war of chemical and biological weapons and is considered the first modern arms control agreement, is a rule of warfare and not a disarmament agreement, and it also has no verification provisions. When the Italian Army used poison gas against the Ethiopian Army in 1935, the Egyptian Army against Yemen in 1967, and Iraq during the war against Iran in the 1980s, it was the use of chemicals in combat that confirmed violation of the protocol. Finally, the Washington Naval Treaty of 1922, which established equipment limitations but never came into force, also had no verification provisions. The battleship ratios and other limits on naval vessels were considered to be easily observable. And even in recent years there have been important arms limitation agreements concluded that contain no comprehensive verification provisions.

The debate about the importance of verification has continued to the present. During the negotiation of the Ottawa Convention on land mines in the late 1990s, a division arose between nations advocating detailed verification and those maintaining that the emerging treaty was humanitarian in character. The latter approach was supported by the International Committee of the Red Cross (ICRC), which argued that what was important was a clear international norm of behavior prohibiting the use of antipersonnel land mines, as opposed to complicated obligations and detailed verification provisions that could have taken a long time to develop and negotiate. Thus there was disagreement on whether the prohibition on land mines should be monitored by classic arms control verification arrangements (as developed in the nuclear age), which involve continuous monitoring, on-site inspections, and reporting requirements, or merely by complaints filed with the United Nations Security Council.[3] The final result was closer to the latter than to the former, and consistent with the approach of the Geneva Protocol of 1925, as described above.

More recently, the United States and Russia have concluded a strategic nuclear arms agreement that does not include any detailed verification issues (see the Strategic Offensive Reductions Treaty [SORT] in Appendix B). Although SORT acknowledges and takes advantage of the comprehensive Strategic Arms Reduction Treaty (START I) verification provisions still in place, the decision to avoid prolonged negotiations to work out new verification procedures was evidence of a new era in U.S.-Russian strategic relations. However, this approach has been criticized by some, especially its lack of provisions to cover the dismantlement and elimination of warheads.

Although verification and enforcement have played an important role in traditional nuclear arms control, the real importance of independent and reliable verification is dictated by the potential significance of violations, which varies depending on the type of weapon that is being limited or prohibited. With nuclear arms control, 99 percent confidence that one's treaty partner is not cheating is sometimes not considered sufficient. However, 50 percent confidence that land mines are no longer being deployed may still be a great benefit to the world community.

Generally speaking, the ICRC approach limiting the use of land mines had been adopted earlier with respect to other modern arms limitation treaties, such as the 1967 Outer Space Treaty and the 1972 Seabed Arms Control Treaty. The first agreement prohibits, among other things, the stationing of nuclear weapons and other WMD in outer space,[4] and the second prohibits the deployment of such weapons on the beds of the high seas.[5] The Environmental Modification Convention of 1977,[6] which prohibited the use of environmental modification techniques such as rainmaking as weapons of war, followed suit.

The Outer Space Treaty does not mention verification. It mandates simply that states parties agree to inform the Secretary-General of the United Nations, the international scientific community, and the public of their activities in outer space. All installations and space vehicles on celestial bodies are open to representatives of other states parties on the basis of reciprocity.

The subject of verification in the negotiation of the Seabed Arms Control Treaty was, by contrast, the subject of intense discussion. Article III is the longest article in the treaty and provides that each state party has the right to verify the activities of other states parties through observation. If after observation reasonable doubts remain about the activities of a party being consistent with the obligations of the treaty, the observing party and the party carrying out the activity are to consult and circulate a report. If it is not clear who is carrying out the activities, the party questioning the activity can consult with other parties in the region and even conduct inspections. If after all this, doubts persist, a party is authorized to refer the matter to the UN Security Council. A party engaged in verification activities under the treaty is authorized to use its "own (national) means" with the assistance of other parties, if desired, as well as appropriate "international procedures" within the framework of the United Nations. All verification activities carried out by a party are to avoid interference with the activities of other states and be consistent with international law. (See Appendix B for details on the Seabed Arms Control Treaty's verification language.)

Risks Associated with Weak or No Verification

The case of the Biological Weapons Convention (BWC) of 1972 is somewhat different and demonstrates the dangers of inadequate verification. It limits arsenals of states by prohibiting not only the use of biological weapons but also their possession.[7] Nevertheless, it also has no verification provisions, only complaint procedures leading to the UN Security Council. But, as with the later Ottawa Convention on land mines, it was believed in 1972 that establishing an international norm of behavior prohibiting the possession of biological weapons was sufficiently important that a treaty should be negotiated despite the lack of feasibility of verifying compliance prior to the use of biological weapons in combat. Also, the United States had formally renounced its own biological weapons stockpile in 1969 and destroyed it in 1970, except for what was deemed necessary for research into defensive measures. Many European countries declared at this time that they did not and would not possess such weapons.

In the ratification hearings before the Senate Foreign Relations Committee in 1974, the executive branch witnesses, Director of the Arms Control and Disarmament Agency Fred Ikle and Chairman of the Joint Chiefs of Staff General George Brown, both addressed their testimony in part to the lack of verification provisions in the BWC. They unequivocally stated to the committee for the record that the BWC was not verifiable but remained in the interests of the United States because of the worldwide norm of behavior established by the convention as well as the U.S. unilateral renunciation.[8] The BWC came into force in 1975.

In March 1980, just weeks before the first review conference of the BWC, it was learned that there had been an explosion in a Soviet laboratory in Sverdlovsk (now Ekaterinburg) that had apparently released deadly anthrax spores and caused a number of deaths. Anthrax is a primary biological weapons agent, and this information suggested that the Soviets were violating the BWC. The United States learned of this violation through essentially intelligence means—interviewing defectors—and it became a big issue. The review conference was held just a few weeks later, and the United States raised this issue with vigor. The Soviets denied the event, of course, and claimed that no one had contracted anthrax; rather the illness was something they called Siberian ulcer. Other than charge and countercharge, not much was accomplished at the BWC Review Conference, but the issue had been raised, and the United States had considerable support from the other BWC parties at the conference. The Sverdlovsk issue was discussed again at the second review conference in 1986. At that conference the United States alleged Soviet involvement in the production, transfer, and use of mycotoxins as weapons of war (the poisonous so-called yellow rain in Southeast Asia) and that the Soviet Union maintained an offensive biological warfare program in direct violation of the BWC. The assertion as to yellow rain was never proven, but the issue of Soviet compliance with the BWC was pursued after the end of the Cold War.[9]

In the early 1990s, irrefutable evidence was finally uncovered that the Soviet Union had secretly and massively violated the BWC and had in place a vast offensive biological weapons development and production establishment. President Boris Yeltsin revealed that the Soviet Union had been in violation of the BWC from the very beginning and had constructed a huge infrastructure for its program. Negotiations with the Russian government in the 1990s led to gradual immobilization of the program and to partial conversion of this infrastructure to peaceful purposes. It also reignited international efforts to create a verification regime for the BWC. However, the international community has yet to devise a verification approach that is both effective and acceptable because of the as yet unacceptably intrusive measures that such verification would entail. This BWC episode demonstrates that effective verification is possible only when it is practical and politically feasible.

But negotiations involving the nuclear weapon systems of the United States and the Soviet Union, the centerpiece of the vast military might each superpower possessed during the Cold War, were another matter. In this arena, an agreement like the BWC without verification would not be tolerated because of the potential strategic advantages through cheating.

While the first agreement of the nuclear age limiting nuclear weapons, the Antarctic Treaty of 1959, did have on-site inspection provisions, this was an anomaly. The Antarctic Treaty was thought of as primarily an environmental protection agreement. It was the negotiations directly affecting the superpower nuclear arsenals during the Cold War arms race that gave rise to the necessity of comprehensive, effective, and reliable verification provisions. Nuclear weapons, after all, were seen as the ultimate guarantor of each side's national security. Biological and chemical weapons, though capable of mass casualties, were not seen as being strategically significant. The United States and the Soviet Union were seemingly engaged in a struggle to the death over mastery of the world, and there was enormous suspicion and lack of trust on both sides. Verification, therefore, became the core issue of all strategic nuclear arms control agreements between the two countries. Without effective verification, the Cold War might not have ended as peacefully as it did, and U.S. and Russian nuclear arsenals, while still far too high, would not be anywhere near as low as they currently are.

2

Soviet Secrecy Fuels the Arms Race and Inhibits Verification

THE UNITED STATES, of course, developed nuclear weapons first and in 1945 demonstrated their terrible power in attacks on Hiroshima and Nagasaki. The Soviet Union acquired nuclear weapons in 1949, only four years later, due in large measure to the efficiency of their atomic spy ring at Los Alamos and in New York.[1] The United States tested a thermonuclear weapon in 1952, and the Soviet Union followed suit in 1953. The vast nuclear arms race was now on in earnest. In the beginning, nuclear weapons were measured in terms of kilotons, an equivalent to 1,000 tons of TNT explosive power; the Hiroshima bomb was 12.5 kilotons, or the equivalent in explosive power of 12,500 tons of TNT. Subsequently, during the Cold War the United States built 72,000 nuclear weapons and possessed at a peak time over 32,000 of them. The Soviet Union built 55,000 nuclear weapons and possessed up to 45,000 for a number of years, while making enough nuclear explosive material for many thousand more weapons.[2]

When the Soviet Union broke the three-year moratorium on nuclear weapons testing in 1961 (see page 22 below), it did so with a blast of 58.6 megatons, the largest nuclear test explosion of all time.[3] To gain an understanding of the destructive power of such weapons, consider that a 9-megaton warhead (the size of the weapon deployed on the largest U.S. strategic missiles in the early 1960s) detonated at the Washington Monument would more or less level Washington, D.C., out to the Beltway—some fifteen miles distant—in every direction.

The United States and the Soviet Union came extremely close to nuclear war during the Cuban missile crisis of 1962. Because of this destructive potential, any agreements between the two superpowers mutually limiting their ultimate weapons would have to be verifiable, or, to use the term developed later, "effectively verifiable," sufficiently reliable to detect in time, if not prevent, cheating. But it would be several decades into the Cold War before independent and reliable verification would be practical and politically acceptable.

The Challenge of Soviet Secrecy

One of the major drivers of the almost absurd intensity of the nuclear arms race—as viewed in retrospect—was the deep suspicion between the two sides compounded by the complete Soviet dedication to secrecy. Indeed, secrecy was a deeply ingrained Russian national characteristic going back centuries. For a long time it was perceived as necessary to hide Russian weakness from the West. Russia had been invaded with devastating results by Sweden (twice), Napoleon, the

German Kaiser, and finally Hitler. In all cases the Russians eventually prevailed, but only after huge losses, the worst coming in World War II. When the Soviet Union finally agreed to a minimal exchange of data on strategic systems in 1978 toward the end of the second Strategic Arms Limitation Talks (SALT II), the Soviet ambassador said to the U.S. ambassador: "Today we are repealing 400 years of Russian history."[4]

An example of this Soviet penchant for secrecy took place in 1970, during SALT I negotiations between the United States and the Soviet Union. The objective of these negotiations was to place initial limits on the central offensive strategic nuclear weapons systems of the two parties and thereby begin bringing the nuclear arms race under control. To help the chief U.S. negotiator, Ambassador Gerard Smith, to make the point that bigger missiles were not necessarily more threatening, one of the U.S. advisers made a chart showing silhouettes of the various ballistic missiles of each side. It demonstrated that though smaller, the U.S. Minuteman and Polaris missiles posed a greater threat than the then current much larger Soviet missiles. The Soviet ambassador gave the chart to his senior general staff officer, who commented only that "the Americans have a good artist." The Soviets refused to engage further.

On another occasion, the representative of the Joint Chiefs of Staff on the U.S. delegation was explaining a new comprehensive U.S. proposal to the Soviet side. In making his presentation, the U.S. representative, General Royal Allison, made use of a map of the Soviet Union that disclosed the location of intercontinental ballistic missile (ICBM) deployments. After Allison's presentation, his Soviet opposite, General Nikolai Ogarchov, took him aside and asked him not to make such a presentation to the Soviet delegation again as "our civilians are not cleared for this information."[5]

Inasmuch as secrecy was part of the cultural history of Russia, this obsession with secrecy was only secondarily an outgrowth of Soviet doctrine. Nevertheless, its persistence made the Cold War far more dangerous. The Cold War playing field was certainly not an even

Vladivostok Naval Base. Reconnaissance satellites imaged all Soviet naval bases in an effort to follow and understand the development, deployment, and capabilities of Soviet naval forces. Credit: DigitalGlobe/Getty Images 57661620

one. The Soviets were able to capitalize on the relatively open U.S. society and news media to learn about U.S. and NATO military capabilities and planning. For example, it became widely known in the early 1960s that the United States was planning to deploy fifty-four Titan II ICBMs and later a thousand Minuteman missiles. The United States, in contrast, had little open information with which to analyze Soviet strategic capabilities and intentions. A similar imbalance existed with regard to information on Soviet and Warsaw Pact conventional forces opposing NATO. As a result, Berlin and Vienna became strategic locations for recruiting and running human agents in an attempt to discern Soviet military capabilities and intentions. Nevertheless, there were military developments and activities taking place deep within the Soviet Union that exceeded what human agents could hope to penetrate and report on.

This lack of critical information led in the 1950s to worst-case analyses in Washington and elsewhere regarding Soviet intentions and capabilities, thereby risking the misdirection of resources and possibly the creation of destabilizing situations. At times, overestimates of Soviet capabilities led the United States and its Allies to plan for military capabilities that were unnecessary. At other times, underestimates of Soviet capabilities led to accusations that the United States was not adequately meeting the threat and actually was losing the arms race. In both cases, political and budgetary battles resulted from the lack of an accurate understanding of the nature of the Soviet threat. In the late 1950s and early 1960s, Western intelligence organizations consequently turned quickly to innovative technical means, such as high-altitude reconnaissance aircraft and satellites, in an effort to detect and monitor hidden activities. They also began to devise new ways of analyzing the intelligence they needed to avoid a hot war that might result from miscalculations of Soviet military capabilities, actions, and intentions.

The missile gap of the late 1950s, when the United States mistakenly perceived that it was behind in missile development and deployments, turned out to be a fable, but it set in motion first the U.S. defense bureaucracy and later the Soviet defense bureaucracy to build large nuclear deterrent forces. This led both countries ultimately to the reckless and unnecessary building of thousands of nuclear-capable strategic ballistic missiles, which could deliver many thousands of nuclear weapons and thereby utterly devastate both countries in a matter of thirty minutes. These systems were maintained on hair-trigger alert and, once launched, could not be recalled.

The understandable inclination in this atmosphere of fear and suspicion to adopt a worst-case stance and assume a maximum threat from the other side pushed both sides to the extreme of nuclear weapons development and deployment as well as to hair-trigger alert and response systems. Sometimes there were mistakes, such as radar early-warning systems registering a missile attack when sighting geese. The commander of the U.S. Strategic Air Command carried a telephone twenty-four hours a day, seven days a week, which he was obligated to answer by the third ring. If he received a call reporting the detection of a Soviet missile attack on the United States, a procedure was in place involving the senior officials of the U.S. national security apparatus and the president, who were to decide within twenty minutes whether to launch strategic nuclear missiles before the detected Soviet missiles arrived. Needless to say, one technical malfunction or human error could lead to Armageddon.

The seriousness of the circumstances was demonstrated at the time of the Cuban missile crisis, when the United States and the Soviet Union—and along with them the rest of the world—were on the brink of nuclear war. Robert McNamara, the secretary of defense at that time, has said many times in later years that the Cuban missile crisis was the best-managed international crisis of the twentieth century, but in reality disaster was avoided by luck. President Kennedy was urged by Congress and the Joint Chiefs of Staff to invade Cuba before the Soviet medium-range nuclear missiles, which could strike as far north as Washington, D.C., became operational. He was assured by his intelligence and military advisers that as of that time there were no Soviet nuclear missiles yet operational. However, Kennedy chose to settle the crisis diplomatically. More than thirty-five years later the United States found out that there were—in addition to twenty nuclear warheads for the medium-range missiles—nine fully operational Soviet short-range nuclear missiles, for which launch authority had already been given by Moscow, which might have been used in the case of a U.S. invasion of the island.[6] It should be noted that in 1962, satellite reconnaissance had recently begun, but it played no role in the crisis; the United States had to rely on aerial reconnaissance for its intelligence.

Earlier, President Eisenhower, recognizing the serious dangers that the developing nuclear arms race combined with Soviet secrecy was creating, sought a way out. The first real summit of the Cold War, the quadripartite Summit Conference, involving the United States, the Soviet Union, the United Kingdom, and France, was held in Geneva, Switzerland, in July 1955. In a speech to the conference on its fourth day, President Eisenhower proposed an agreement between the United States and the Soviet Union permitting aerial reconnaissance flights over each other's territory so as to end the worst-case assumptions of each side regarding the military capabilities and intentions of the other side.[7] When President Eisenhower made his proposal, the lights suddenly were extinguished in the conference hall. Despite the accidental theatrics, the Soviet Union rejected Eisenhower's proposal, claiming that the overflights by reconnaissance aircraft could be used for extensive spying. As a result of this rejection and partly because high-flying overflight aircraft soon became available, with reconnaissance satellites becoming operational in the next decade, this idea of open skies lay dormant for a generation, until it was successfully revived by President George H. W. Bush in 1989 at the end of the Cold War.[8]

Early Efforts to Negotiate a Ban on Nuclear Testing

Early disarmament initiatives included efforts to negotiate an international agreement to end nuclear weapons tests, which were seen as fueling the arms race and causing health hazards. Negotiations began in the Subcommittee of Five (the United States, the United Kingdom, Canada, France, and the Soviet Union) of the United Nations Disarmament Commission in May 1955, when the Soviet Union included the discontinuance of nuclear weapons tests in its proposals.[9] The Subcommittee of Five was the quadripartite group plus Canada, which at the time was considered a very advanced nuclear state. Several events had raised concern in the international community over nuclear weapon tests, but the inadequacies of verification soon became a significant stumbling block to a comprehensive ban on testing.

The United States, in November 1952, and the Soviet Union, in August of the following year, had exploded their first hydrogen devices. In March 1954, the United States detonated an experimental nuclear device in the South Pacific that had an area of dangerous fallout greatly exceeding predicted estimates and extending far beyond the warning area. Indeed, the yield of the device, some fifteen megatons, was approximately twice the anticipated explosive yield. A Japanese fishing vessel, the *Lucky Dragon*, was accidentally contaminated, and its crew suffered from radiation sickness (with one crewman dying), as did the inhabitants of an atoll in the area. In another such incident, rain containing radioactive debris from a Soviet hydrogen bomb test fell on Japan. Concern about radioactive fallout, the prospect of ever more powerful explosions, and the potential for the byproducts of such explosives to enter the food chain (particularly the isotope strontium-90 in milk) spurred efforts to halt testing. Even amid widespread international concern, the negotiation of a treaty providing the first constraints on nuclear weapon tests extended over an eight-year period (until 1963) and involved complex technical problems, related to both verification and the difficulties of reconciling deep-seated differences in U.S. and Soviet approaches to arms control, secrecy, and security.[10]

On the question of verification measures, the Western powers were determined to ensure that no militarily significant agreement would be vulnerable to clandestine violation. This applied particularly to the potential for underground nuclear explosions, which they believed could be conducted in secret. The central weapons of national security in the Cold War were involved in nuclear test ban negotiations, as well as in related nuclear arms control efforts, and the United States and its Allies considered it simply too dangerous to accept simple pledges from the Soviet Union without the means of knowing that the limitations would be observed. They also believed that such pledges without verification would be misleading, creating illusions of secure progress toward nuclear disarmament. The Soviet Union, given its commitment to secrecy and relatively easy access to U.S. policy deliberations and military activities, insisted that formal verification measures were not necessary—and therefore Soviet territory did not need to be inspected.

The Soviets argued that it would be impossible for any state to conduct an underground nuclear weapon test without being detected and continued to press for an immediate suspension of nuclear weapons tests. However, the United States urged agreement on a control or verification system as a necessary accompanying measure. The United States was unwilling to accept the basic propositions of the Soviet Union that a nuclear weapon test ban could be agreed to first and verification arrangements negotiated and instituted subsequently, or to accept mutual indefinite test suspensions, which would be tantamount to endorsing an unverifiable test ban.

However, in 1958 as part of an effort to jump-start negotiations on a treaty banning all nuclear tests, President Eisenhower announced a one-year moratorium on U.S. nuclear weapons tests, and the Soviet Union followed suit. The United States and the Soviet Union continued this policy beyond the one-year limit, but after France conducted its first nuclear test in the Sahara Desert in 1960, the Soviet Union broke the moratorium in 1961 with the largest nuclear explosion of all time. The United States responded by resuming a vigorous test series of its own.[11]

Thereafter, verification and inspection issues remained the principal stumbling blocks to moving forward with the test ban as well as other negotiations. The United States wanted on-site inspections and unmanned seismic detection stations on Soviet territory. The Soviets eventually accepted both in principle, but the two sides could not agree on the associated numbers: the United States wanted the right to conduct up to seven on-site inspections per year, while the Soviets would agree to only three. The same was true for remote sensors, unmanned seismic instruments that could be connected to a monitoring station outside the Soviet Union: the principle of their use was now agreed upon, but the numbers were not.

The United States and the United Kingdom, in high-level correspondence with the Soviet Union, then sought to arrange three-power talks. Finally, on June 10, 1963, in a speech at American University, President John F. Kennedy announced that agreement had been reached to hold three-power meetings on the test ban in Moscow. In order to bypass the stalemate over verification and at the same time address the environmental issues associated with testing, President Kennedy proposed a treaty banning nuclear tests in the atmosphere, underwater, and in outer space, but not underground, where the disputed verification issues were unresolved.

Limited Test Ban Treaty

Thus, as a result of the inability to agree on the parameters for utilization of technical verification systems (unmanned seismic stations) as well as on-site inspections, the parties settled in 1963 on an agreement that was essentially an environmental protection agreement rather than a security treaty. Nevertheless, the Limited Test Ban (LTBT) was a landmark treaty since it was the first agreement to limit nuclear test activities. Also, it contained language in its preamble calling for a complete ban on nuclear weapons tests that eventually led to the negotiation and signing of the Comprehensive Test Ban Treaty (CTBT) in 1996.[12]

However, in leaving open the opportunity for underground nuclear weapons tests, the LTBT made possible a large increase in their number. The annual number of U.S. nuclear tests, for example, tripled after 1962. The Jackson Safeguards, promoted by Senator Henry Jackson during the ratification proceedings and attached to the Senate resolution of ratification of the LTBT, mandated that this would happen as a condition of ratification of the treaty (and the end of atmospheric testing). These safeguards called for, among other things, improved technical verification systems and a vigorous underground nuclear test program. Another byproduct of the Jackson Safeguards was the Vela satellite system, designed to detect nuclear tests in the atmosphere.

The ending of atmospheric nuclear weapon tests eliminated the threat to the food chain and, among other things, ensured that no longer would there be a buildup of strontium-90 in milk products, but the LTBT did nothing to control the nuclear arms race, which considerably escalated after 1962. While it was not possible to conduct blasts of 58.6 megatons underground, there could be and were tests of up to 2 megatons carried out underground, which, when carried out properly, entailed no radiation leaking into the atmosphere. This level of testing proved to be more than sufficient for the requirements of U.S. and Soviet nuclear weapon test programs, including those to develop the explosive components of multiple independently targetable reentry vehicles (MIRVs). And with the advent of MIRVs in 1970, deployed nuclear weapons vastly increased in numbers and, although smaller in explosive yields, became more accurate. Studies indicated that an area target hit, for example, by several half-megaton weapons delivered by MIRVs would be more devastated than if hit by a single multimegaton warhead.

Threshold Test Ban Treaty

Following the signing of the LTBT, a long period ensued, approximately thirty years, when no significant progress was made in controlling nuclear weapon testing. For years the United States and the Soviet Union did not even try. In 1974, however, the United States and Soviet Union signed the Threshold Test Ban Treaty (TTBT), which limited underground nuclear weapons tests to 150 kilotons, a little more than ten times the size of the Hiroshima explosion.[13] And in 1976, the two parties signed a companion Peaceful Nuclear Explosions Treaty (PNET), which permitted nuclear explosions for peaceful purposes, such as for digging canals, natural gas stimulation, and the like, but imposed the same yield limit.[14] In terms of verification, the TTBT contained some limited data exchange provisions, and the PNET contained some minor on-site inspection obligations. However, the two treaties came into force only in 1990, after the negotiation of highly complex and detailed on-site inspection protocols amending the two treaties.[15] Thus, while the two test ban treaties were informally observed for many years, verification of a yield threshold by remote seismic measurements was inherently uncertain. Even a test explosion of 100 kilotons, well below the limitation, had an uncertainty factor that created the possibility under certain conditions, as far as verification was concerned, of an explosion well above 150 kilotons. The two treaties were highly controversial in the United States, and they could not be brought into force until the end of the Cold War made intrusive on-site inspection arrangements possible.

Thus, the efforts to slow the arms race by prohibiting further nuclear weapon test explosions in the 1950s and early 1960s essentially failed over the issue of verification. In 1962, existing national means—listening and monitoring stations in third countries—were not considered effective enough to monitor a complete or comprehensive nuclear test ban. And the negotiating parties could not get together on an agreed number of permitted in-country unmanned monitoring devices and on-site inspections. The verification uncertainties associated with the TTBT in the 1970s only underscored this problem.

Comprehensive Nuclear Test Ban Treaty

Even though a treaty banning all nuclear weapons tests was considered the principal "quid" for the "quo" of the commitment of the current 183 nations around the world not to acquire nuclear weapons, pursuant to the 1968 Nuclear Non-Proliferation Treaty (NPT)—the centerpiece of international security—the United States and the Soviet Union remained so suspicious of one another that substantial limitations on nuclear weapon testing remained elusive until after the end of the Cold War. The CTBT was finally signed in 1996, and it includes remote technical monitoring by national and international sensors as well as on-site inspections. However, it still has not entered into force because of its rejection by the U.S. Senate in 1999, in part because of continuing suspicions regarding Russian testing activity at their test site on the islands of Novaya Zemlya and ongoing resistance by several other key countries.[16]

Since the end of the Cold War, the United States and several other countries have periodically voiced concern about Russian testing activities because Russia, along with China, has traditionally been more secretive and less willing to make its testing practices and activities public. In early March 1996, when the CTBT negotiations were entering their final phase, the news media reported that U.S. intelligence suspected that the Russians had secretly exploded a nuclear device, thereby breaking their four-year unilateral moratorium on testing. Although some believed it unlikely that the Soviets had tested and U.S. officials reportedly declared the information to be inconclusive, others voiced certainty that the Russians had tested.[17] In response to repeated démarches and requests that it be more transparent, Moscow has consistently said only that it conducts activity at its test site in a manner consistent with its international obligations. On March 7, 1996, Grigory Berdennikov, the Russian ambassador to the Conference on Disarmament in Geneva, which was conducting the CTBT negotiations, formally stated in a plenary meeting that "Russia has not conducted a single nuclear explosion, rigorously observing the moratorium it has declared."[18] Nevertheless, this episode demonstrates that some suspicions regarding Russian activities continue even after the end of the Cold War, which reinforces the need for effective monitoring—national, international, or both.

3

U.S. Efforts to Understand Soviet Military
Forces and Capabilities

IT DID NOT TAKE LONG for the optimism of wartime cooperation

between the United States and the Soviet Union against Nazi Ger-

many to slip back into the pre–World War II pattern of suspicion

and hostility. Gone was the common enemy, and, using its inter-

national network of Communist parties and sympathizers, the

Soviet Communist Party began a full-fledged offensive to win the

hearts and minds of the rest of the world over to communism. With numerically superior Warsaw Pact ground forces threatening Western Europe, along with the Communist victory in China and the North Korean offensive into the South, the United States found itself in the late 1940s and through the 1950s in a global struggle with a rising Communist menace that possessed nuclear weapons and an increasing capability to strike U.S. Allies and the continental United States.

U.S. policy makers were in desperate need of better information about the military capabilities and intentions of Stalin and his successors. More and better intelligence was needed about what the Soviets were doing both in Eastern Europe and deep within their own territory to avoid wasting resources on unneeded military capabilities and inadvertently starting World War III through ignorance and miscalculation. This meant that the United States needed human agents with better access as well as new remote technical monitoring capabilities to detect and monitor what the Soviets were doing with their military forces, both conventional and nuclear.[1] These Cold War policy requirements led to the U.S. Intelligence Community becoming the world's largest, most diverse, and most capable national foreign intelligence service (see Appendix F for details).

U.S. INTELLIGENCE COMMUNITY

The U.S. Intelligence Community (IC) refers to those executive branch agencies and organizations that conduct a variety of intelligence activities to satisfy the requirements of the policy community. Many of these organizations were instrumental in developing, with the help of U.S. industry, and utilizing the intelligence required to understand Soviet military forces during the Cold War. These intelligence capabilities remain critical to efforts to monitor military forces under various arms control agreements.

The IC is currently comprised of sixteen organizations.

Those that focus, at least in part, on military and strategic nuclear issues include the Central Intelligence Agency; the National Security Agency; the Defense Intelligence Agency; the Bureau of Intelligence and Research of the Department of State; the Army, Navy, Marine Corps, and Air Force intelligence services; the National Geospatial-Intelligence Agency; the National Reconnaissance Office; and the Department of Energy. The others include the Federal Bureau of Investigation (for domestic counterintelligence and counterterrorism activities); the Department of Homeland Security; the Coast Guard; the Department of the Treasury; and the Drug Enforcement Administration.

Members of the IC advise the Director of National Intelligence (DNI) through their representation in a number of specialized bodies. These include the new National Counterterrorism Center and the National Intelligence Council. The Intelligence Reform Act of 2004 created the new DNI position to provide better coordination and communication among the various components of the IC in order to meet the intelligence challenges of the twenty-first century.

Bomber and Missile Gaps

The risk of such miscalculation was demonstrated most vividly in the latter half of the 1950s with the so-called bomber and missile gaps, which led critics of the Eisenhower administration to accuse it of underestimating, first, the size and capabilities of the Soviet strategic bomber force and, later, of Soviet long-range missile forces. Such misunderstandings of the threat created the possibility of overreacting in terms of U.S. policy and military decisions, particularly regarding investment in the development and deployment of new and larger military forces.

The bomber gap was the direct result of attaché reporting from a

Soviet military parade in 1954, during which the Soviets deceived Western observers by flying their latest intercontinental-range jet "Bison" bombers repeatedly over Red Square in various formations to make it look as though their inventory of these bombers was much larger than it was. This led the attachés, and others, to exaggerate the number of aircraft the Soviets had in their inventory.[2] A few years later, following the launch of Sputnik, accusations of a missile gap became a campaign issue used by the Democrats to accuse the Eisenhower administration of falling behind in missile technology and the deployment of intercontinental ballistic missiles (ICBMs).[3] Thus, the Eisenhower and all subsequent U.S. administrations have looked to the Intelligence Community to provide improved collection and analysis in order to better understand Soviet strategic forces and manage the U.S.-Soviet arms race.

Air Reconnaissance Systems

In the 1950s, one of the first efforts to monitor Soviet military activity deep inside the Soviet Union involved high-flying balloons carrying cameras. The obvious difficulty with this system was ensuring that the balloons followed the intended track, took the desired pictures, and were retrieved by the right people. This effort was at best hit-and-miss and did not provide reliable data on Soviet forces.[4] As one of the analysts involved subsequently related, U.S. analysts often did not know where the pictures were taken, and none of the pictures captured significant information.

Early attempts to remotely collect information on Soviet military developments on a consistent basis were limited initially to modified military aircraft flying off the coasts of the Soviet Union and along the NATO-Warsaw Pact frontier in Europe. However, such efforts could not reach much beyond the peripheral areas. It facilitated the monitoring of ground, air, and naval forces facing NATO, but no strategic bomber and missile fabrication plants, test facilities, and

bases were located in those areas. Moreover, some of the reconnaissance aircraft were shot down by Soviet interceptors, with
Moscow claiming that the U.S. aircraft had entered Soviet air space
in violation of international law. Consequently, the capability to probe
the Soviet interior with less risk to U.S. personnel was desperately
needed, and an effort was launched in the first half of the 1950s to
produce an appropriate aircraft. After the failure of Eisenhower's open
skies proposal at the 1955 Summit Conference in Geneva, the United
States began conducting reconnaissance overflights of the Soviet
Union in 1956 with its new secret, very high altitude aircraft referred
to as the U-2.

When the CIA came into existence in 1947, no one foresaw that
it would undertake a major program of overhead reconnaissance as
part of its clandestine collection responsibilities. Traditionally, the military services had been responsible for air reconnaissance, and flights
deep into unfriendly territory had taken place only during wartime.
Indeed, the U.S. Air Force was in the process of developing a high-
altitude reconnaissance aircraft that would be able to conduct missions over the Soviet Union, but the White House was concerned that
the loss of a U.S. military aircraft deep over Soviet territory would
be interpreted by the Soviets as an act of war. Military reconnaissance
flights along the periphery of the Soviet Union had already been costly
in terms of lives lost. The CIA soon found itself responsible for the
new covert overflight program, which led to the development and operation of two new aircraft, the U-2 and the SR-71.

The U-2 Program

In the mid-1950s, the Eisenhower administration launched the
design and construction of a new type of nonmilitary manned reconnaissance airplane that could fly high enough to avoid Soviet anti-
aircraft batteries and interceptors, fly far enough to cover the areas
of the Soviet Union of interest, and return. It would need to be

U-2. This unique aircraft was secretly developed by the Intelligence community in conjunction with private industry to satisfy policy requirements for more comprehensive and detailed information on Soviet military developments and capabilities. Credit: Robert McMahon Photographs

equipped with cameras that could function at the required altitude. This called for new concepts, creative contractor expertise and support, and access to foreign bases. After a brief design competition, the CIA turned to Lockheed Aircraft's Skunk Works and its chief designer, Kelly Johnson, who produced the U-2 aircraft on time and under budget.[5]

The president insisted that the program be manned by civilians and operated in greatest secrecy. Therefore, primary management and operational responsibility for the program was given to the CIA, with support from the U.S. Air Force in terms of transport and foreign basing. By the latter half of the 1950s, U-2 operations over the Soviet Union were in full swing using bases around the world. These flights quickly provided, among other things, clear evidence that the bomber gap claims had been incorrect—the result of overestimating Soviet capabilities based on insufficient intelligence data.[6]

The Soviet Union considered these flights to be attempts at espionage; the United States considered them essential reconnaissance without which, given the closed Soviet society, the nuclear arms race would spin completely out of control (as it nearly did five years later during the Cuban missile crisis of 1962). Eisenhower was increasingly concerned that a U-2 would eventually be brought down, since the Soviets were making a concerted effort to improve their intercept capabilities. Finally, this happened; U-2 overflights of the Soviet interior ceased in May 1960, after the aircraft of Gary Powers was shot down by an advanced Soviet surface-to-air missile. After complaining about these overflights but helpless to stop them, the Soviets finally had developed an interceptor missile with sufficient range and altitude to hit the high-flying aircraft. The incident was big news and the excuse Soviet premier Khrushchev used to break up the Paris Summit Conference with President Eisenhower in May 1960.

Nevertheless, for the few years that U-2 missions over the Soviet Union were possible, the United States was able to gain new insights into selected Soviet military production and force capabilities, such as the number of Soviet heavy bombers. Comprehensive coverage of these targets, however, would have to wait for the advent of satellite imagery. Meanwhile, the U-2 aircraft went on to serve for more than twenty years in various other theaters, including the Middle East, Asia, and the Caribbean. It was the U-2, after all, that was able in 1962 to provide the definitive proof that the Soviets were installing offensive, medium-range ballistic missiles in Cuba. The United States used the U-2 photographs to show the UN Security Council that the Soviets had been lying about their military activities on that island. And in 1973, the United Nations requested the services of U-2 aircraft to monitor the truce between Israel and its Arab neighbors following the Yom Kippur War. Variants of the U-2 continue to be used to monitor crises around the world.[7] Today, new generations of U-2s perform high-altitude weather research, earth resources surveys, and aerial mapping, as well as strategic reconnaissance.

In the 1940s, Edward Land developed the Polaroid instant camera and founded the Polaroid Company, but he also played an important role in the development of the incredibly capable photographic devices that were carried on the U-2 aircraft, its successor, the SR-71, and later on the first U.S. artificial earth reconnaissance satellites. After the Soviets shot down the U-2 aircraft, it was revealed in news reports of the time that the camera on board the U-2s had the capability from twenty miles in the air to distinguish tennis balls on a tennis court. It was truly a new age.

However, U-2 flights raised a fundamental principle of international law. For many centuries an unjustified incursion across a state's international border by another state has been considered a breach of sovereignty—a violation of international law. And a state's sovereign territory is not limited to its land area but includes the airspace above its territory. Thus the unauthorized flight of one state's aircraft into the sovereign airspace of another state is a violation of international law. But the question is, how high does a state's sovereign airspace extend? Since the 1967 Outer Space Treaty was signed, outer space as well as all bodies such as the moon are recognized as not subject to national jurisdiction. Space is the province of humanity— *res commun*—not subject to national appropriation, similar to the high seas. Before the advent of the treaty this was the view of most commentators on international law, but some states argued that national sovereignty extended indefinitely out into space. However, the prevailing view argued that national airspace ended either where airlift was no longer possible or where the atmosphere substantially ended, around one hundred kilometers above the earth. This was above the altitude capabilities of the U-2.

When Premier Khrushchev walked out of the Paris Summit Conference, he accused the United States of violating international law and conducting espionage. Embarrassed and realizing the dangers associated with continued overflights, Eisenhower terminated the U-2 flights over the Soviet Union. Perhaps coincidentally, reports began to spread of a missile gap between the United States and the Soviet Union in which the Soviets had the advantage, to the national security detriment of the United States. This became a major issue in the 1960 presidential campaign between Senator John F. Kennedy and Vice President Richard M. Nixon. After the Kennedy administration took office and as a result of intelligence obtained by the new artificial earth satellite reconnaissance capabilities, the so-called missile gap was proven to be nonexistent.

SR-71 Program

Realizing the limitations of the U-2 even before the downing of Powers's aircraft, U.S. experts researched ways to make the aircraft more survivable. The studies led them to conclude that an entirely new aircraft would be required to meet the speed and altitude requirements of survivability. Once again following a brief period of competition, the United States turned to Kelly Johnson and his Skunk Works to develop the new aircraft. And the CIA again took the lead in ironing out some of the key technical issues before turning the program over to the U.S. Air Force to operate the aircraft. This led in 1962 to the development managed by the CIA of the A-12 Oxcart, which was then used by the Air Force in its SR-71 configuration for U.S. military and intelligence reconnaissance in various parts of the world for four decades. No one has subsequently developed a more capable high-altitude reconnaissance aircraft.[8]

Like the U-2, the SR-71 contributed to international peacekeeping efforts in the Middle East and assisted U.S. forces in Southeast Asia and elsewhere. However, the U.S. halt in reconnaissance flights over

The SR-71. This highly capable aircraft was secretly developed as a follow-on to
the U-2 in an effort to compensate for the vulnerabilities of the latter. Because
of President Eisenhower's promise to suspend aerial overflights of the USSR
following the U-2 incident in 1960, this remarkable aircraft was never used to
overfly the USSR. Credit: Robert McMahan Photographs

the Soviet Union in 1960 limited the SR-71's contribution to monitoring Soviet military developments from the USSR's periphery. Moreover, its capabilities were no match for what was being developed in
the realm of satellite reconnaissance capabilities for monitoring from
space activities deep inside the Soviet Union.

Satellite Reconnaissance Programs

Even in the 1950s it was recognized that, despite the fantastic advancements demonstrated by the U-2 and SR-71, manned aircraft would be inadequate to meet policy-maker needs over the longer term. Thus, in the late 1950s, even before the U-2 shoot-down in 1960, the Eisenhower administration launched a serious effort to develop an artificial earth satellite reconnaissance capability that would not have the vulnerabilities or limitations of the manned aircraft programs. It took numerous attempts to get a satellite system to work as designed, and the initial images taken, because of the high altitude, were not of the same quality as the U-2 photographs. Nevertheless, work continued and quickly led, under the Corona program, to refinements in the cameras and targeting capabilities of the satellites. Moreover, the first successful Corona mission, in the late summer of 1960, provided more usable photos than all of the U-2 flights over the Soviet Union combined. And this program set the stage for further advancements in satellite reconnaissance that would, within the following decade, provide sufficient capability to make the remote monitoring of Soviet conventional and strategic forces good enough to serve as the basis for verifying arms control agreements.[9]

The space age had begun in 1957 with the Soviet launch of Sputnik, the world's first artificial earth satellite. Responses around the world varied, but in that same year there had been a worldwide influenza epidemic and the usual political crisis in the French government during the waning days of the Fourth Republic. A French newspaper of the day recognized these events with a banner headline: "Crise, Crise, Crise, Grippe, Grippe, Grippe, Beep, Beep, Beep." The third reference was to Sputnik 1, the new Soviet earth satellite, which emitted a beeping signal. Even U.S. Secretary of Defense Charles Wilson referred to it only as a "nice, technical trick," but it was clear to many that a new age had begun.[10] The capability of the early U.S. satellites, with respect to both the onboard photographic equipment and the maneuverability of the satellites, was a closely guarded secret. And despite its early lead with Sputnik, the Soviet Union lagged behind in these technologies.

At the United Nations and elsewhere, the Soviets, likening reconnaissance by satellites to that by the U-2 aircraft, routinely denounced the operation of the satellites by the United States as a violation of international law and accused the United States of espionage. U.S. satellites made frequent passes over the Soviet Union, taking photographs of Soviet military installations, most important the bases for the growing number of ICBMs, which were capable of delivering nuclear warheads against the United States. In the early years these Soviet ICBMs were deployed on above-ground launchers easily captured in photographs; later ICBMs were deployed in underground silos so as to be less vulnerable to a first strike. But the increasing capability of U.S. reconnaissance satellites could still easily detect these silo launcher complexes. Over the years, the resolution of the satellite cameras improved to an optical resolution of less than a meter. While the precise resolution of today's imaging satellites remains classified, the United States is generally thought to have optical satellites with resolutions down to a few inches.

During these first years, out of frustration because of their inability to hide their deployed ICBMs, Soviet ICBM crewmen wrote crude Anglo-Saxon epithets in the snow near their missiles. Gradually, however, the Soviet Union developed a similar capability and launched its first reconnaissance satellite in 1962. Within a few years, these and other technical accomplishments made nuclear weapons treaty monitoring and verification feasible for both sides and facilitated the successful SALT I negotiations in the early 1970s, which put the first significant brakes on the rampaging U.S.-Soviet nuclear arms race.

Technical Challenges and Achievements

The successful launch and orbiting of photoreconnaissance satellites was a challenging endeavor and a credit to the efforts of U.S. industry, the CIA, and the U.S. Air Force, a success achieved despite intense interagency rivalry and fighting. It took four years of intense and frustrating effort under the Corona program to successfully build, launch, orbit, and recover photos from a satellite in orbit. The achievement in the late 1950s of an ICBM-level of propulsion made it possible to launch satellites into orbit. However, from February 1959 through June 1960, a dozen U.S. attempts were made to launch and orbit a photoreconnaissance satellite—all failures! One problem after another plagued the program. Its ultimate success was a testimony to the dedication and perseverance of those involved, both industrial contractors and government officials. And Washington's continued support of the program, despite the costly setbacks, was a reminder of the urgent policy requirement for better information on the Soviet Union.

Several important books have touched on the program's challenges. In *Secret Empire: Eisenhower, the CIA, and the Hidden Story of America's Space Espionage*, Philip Taubman recounts early U.S. efforts to develop a space-based photoreconnaissance system. In *The Man Who Kept the Secrets: Richard Helms and the CIA*, Thomas Powers describes how the U-2 aircraft overflights of the Soviet Union operated by the CIA were brought to an end by the 1960 downing of Gary Powers's U-2, and also points out that the CIA had been working for some years on a reconnaissance space satellite program led by the Development Project Staff in the Office of the Deputy Director for Science. The CIA had picked up the program in its early days from the Air Force. Continuing refinement of the camera's capability, Thomas Powers relates, made it possible to obtain photographs from satellites 150 kilometers or more in space that had a resolution as good as that of the photographs taken by the U-2.

This new capability represented a true revolution. Intelligence collection by reconnaissance satellites improved enormously American knowledge of Soviet military capabilities and economic strength: "Every square inch of Soviet territory was opened to American eyes."[11] Eventually, as indicated, the Soviets developed comparable systems of their own. The technical challenges and bureaucratic battles sur-

rounding these U.S. technical developments are well described in Jeffrey
Richelson's *Wizards of Langley*.

Early satellites took pictures for a few days and then jettisoned capsules containing the exposed film that reentered the atmosphere and
floated toward the surface of the earth with the aid of a parachute. If
all went well, the capsules were recovered midair by U.S. Air Force
aircraft, flown to Washington, and then developed and carefully analyzed by intelligence experts. Thus, there was a time lag between the
taking of the pictures and their availability and analysis, an undesirable
but unavoidable aspect of the process at the time. The early satellites
had a single return capsule, but later models had multiple capsules,
allowing the satellite to stay in orbit for a longer period of time. In
the mid-1970s, the United States began orbiting satellites able to
transmit images electronically, thus dispensing with the need to send
back film and thereby also providing nearly real-time satellite imagery
to analysts, military commanders, and policy makers. This capability originally had been envisioned in the 1950s, but technology was
not then sufficiently advanced to make it a reality.[12]

The advent of a system that made possible obtaining quality
imagery and transmitting the data back to earth within minutes permitted those responsible for being alert to potential hostilities, prepar-
ing military plans, or monitoring Soviet strategic forces under various
arms control agreements to do their jobs with more up-to-date and
therefore reliable information. However, potential adversaries could
still counter detection with concealment, denial, and deception. Efforts
to develop day/night and all-weather reconnaissance technologies were
part of the response to counter such concealment activities.

More recently, there have been reports that the Intelligence Community has launched the Future Imagery Architecture Program,
designed to give the United States a much larger fleet of reconnaissance satellites. Instead of four or five large and expensive imagery
satellites in orbit at one time, it is envisioned there will be a dozen
or so smaller, less expensive photo and radar-imaging satellites in orbit,
thereby providing more continuous and comprehensive coverage and

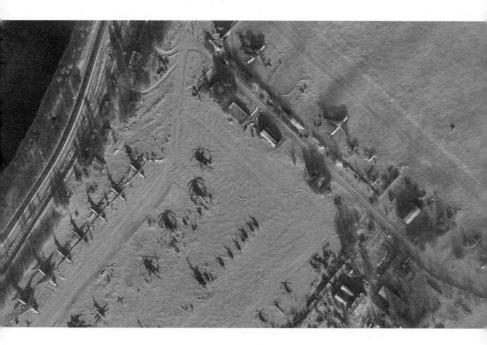

Ramenskoye Air Field. Reconnaissance satellites imaged all Soviet air bases in an effort to follow and understand the development, deployment, and capabilities of Soviet military aircraft. Credit: DigitalGlobe/Getty Images 57661611

allowing the United States to monitor trouble spots around the world without the gaps associated with a smaller number of satellites. Meanwhile, the United States, along with other countries, is also purchasing an increasing amount of high-quality commercial satellite imagery for certain uses. However, it remains critical for the Intelligence Community to operate its own satellites and control what they image in order to meet the fluid and time-sensitive requirements of military commanders and senior policy makers in Washington.[13]

Monitoring Nuclear Weapons Testing Programs

Along with the reconnaissance efforts against the strategic nuclear forces of the Soviet Union, the United States was also working in the early Cold War years on the ability to detect and analyze efforts by other countries to develop and test nuclear devices. Debris from explosions transported by wind currents and collected in the atmosphere was soon deemed to be the best indicator of nuclear explosions, especially from nuclear devices exploded above ground. Because of the prevailing winds around the earth, it was recognized that sooner or later evidence of a Soviet nuclear explosion, for example, would be detectable beyond the Soviet Union's Pacific Coast border. Consequently, the United States began flying long-range reconnaissance aircraft along the Kamchatka Peninsula, and in 1949 it detected evidence of the first Soviet nuclear explosion, confirming the end of the U.S. monopoly on nuclear weapons.

In subsequent years, the United States and other nations learned that their seismological stations, developed principally to monitor earthquakes, could also be used to monitor underground nuclear explosions. Soon technologies were developed to monitor shock waves from nuclear explosions in the oceans using underwater sensors and in the atmosphere using ground-based and space-based sensors. However, these techniques were able to provide indications only that a large explosive test had taken place, not definitive data upon which to confirm that the explosion had been nuclear. The smoking gun for nuclear tests proved to be air sampling by sensors on aircraft or at monitoring stations on the ground that are designed to detect radionuclide particulate or gases (see the text box "Radionuclide Monitoring"). A combination of these various techniques formed the basis of what became the U.S. Atomic Energy Detection System, the backbone of U.S. efforts to monitor nuclear testing around the world (see Appendix D). These techniques were also incorporated into the International Monitoring System (IMS) established by the international community to implement the Comprehensive Nuclear Test Ban Treaty (see Appendix E).[14]

RADIONUCLIDE MONITORING

Certain gases (known as noble gases, such as xenon) that can be released after a nuclear explosion, along with particulate matter (e.g., soil that has been irradiated by a nuclear explosion and dispersed), are the elements collected by radionuclide monitoring systems. The detection of specific radionuclides uniquely identifies the source of the gas or particulates as a nuclear explosion rather than as having come from, for example, a nuclear power plant. Radionuclide detection is therefore considered the only smoking gun in terms of evidence of a nuclear explosion; the other collection techniques (i.e., seismic, hydroacoustic, and infrasound) can indicate only that some type of an explosion has occurred.

There were relatively few radionuclide collectors in existence at the time of the Comprehensive Nuclear Test Ban Treaty negotiations in the mid-1990s; only countries most concerned about monitoring nuclear explosions had invested in them. A large number of monitoring stations have been built around the world as part of the IMS since the CTBT negotiations.

Nonetheless, the detection, characterization, and identification of all nuclear tests, even with proven techniques, have not always been successful. For example, a mysterious bright flash was detected by a U.S. Vela satellite over the South Atlantic in 1979. It was assumed by many to be a South African nuclear test, but it could never be proven through technical data. However, following the change in South African governments, some officials acknowledged that the flash had actually been a joint Israeli–South African test.[15] Similarly, the United States detected preparations for Indian and Pakistani tests in 1995, which permitted the United States to prevent tests at that time.[16] However, it missed the preparations for the Indian tests in May 1998, although it detected the actual tests. In retrospect, it seems clear that the Indians had learned after 1995 how to beat U.S. reconnaissance satellites by successfully concealing their subsequent test preparation activities.[17]

Estimating Soviet Strategic Nuclear Force Capabilities

Intelligence support to policy makers does not stop with the collection of critical data from human or technical sources. Indeed, much of the data collected by technical means is unintelligible to most people unless it is properly processed and analyzed by experts. Photo interpreters, for example, must use careful mensuration and comparison to understand what has been captured by aircraft or space-based imagery systems. Similarly, seismographic and electronic signals data, such as telemetry, must be converted into a form that can be understood.

In the case of the Cuban missile crisis, alert photo interpreters identified crates both in Cuba and on ships that matched those associated with particular Soviet strike aircraft and medium-range ballistic missiles. Moreover, they noticed that the military installations being constructed included soccer fields rather than baseball diamonds, which indicated that the troops were likely Russian rather than Cuban despite Havana's claims. And, as mentioned, it was the photography from the U-2 reconnaissance aircraft that provided the silver bullet U.S. ambassador Adlai Stevenson used to show the world that the Soviets had, in fact, deployed medium-range missiles in Cuba in an effort to redress the U.S.-Soviet strategic nuclear imbalance.

Most U.S. Intelligence Community analysis had, however, concluded during the summer that the Soviets would not deploy such missiles in Cuba given their fear of the anticipated reaction from the United States. In a succession of National Intelligence Estimates (NIEs) over the late summer and early fall of 1962, Intelligence Community analysts explored potential Soviet actions, including nuclear missile deployments, but they concluded that the Soviets would not deploy such missiles. In the end, only Director of Central Intelligence John McCone believed that the Soviets would take such a chance, and he informed the White House of his view. As it turned out, he called it correctly.[18]

During the Cold War, the Intelligence Community's analysis of Soviet strategic nuclear force capabilities and intentions was a high priority for both the Executive Branch and Congress. The Department of Defense in particular was responsible for planning and deploying comparable U.S. forces, and Congress gave careful oversight to weapons procurement activities. Intelligence analysis was provided in the forms of detailed baseline descriptions of force size, characteristics, and capabilities, assessments of current and evolving activities and capabilities, and estimates of future force size and capabilities. The latter, normally prepared as NIEs, were critical for Defense planners, who had to plan for future threats in a situation where it might take a decade for a new U.S. weapon system to advance from concept to the field. The Defense Department and Congress therefore called for rigorous and continuous analysis, which resulted in the production of annual NIEs in an effort to be as current as possible in the U.S. understanding of where the Soviets were headed and to protect the United States from strategic surprise. While forecasts five to ten years out were critical, it was difficult to deliver accurate projections given the uncertainties and long time lines involved. This led to significant debates within the Intelligence Community, which in turn resulted in alternative views regarding how Soviet forces would evolve. It also led to criticisms of the accuracy of the estimates from outside the government, which at times became politicized, such as occurred during the mid-1970s with the A/B Team episode and assertions of an impending U.S. strategic vulnerability.

The Soviets had reacted aggressively to the humiliation of the Cuban missile crisis by launching a massive buildup of its offensive intercontinental strike forces, especially large land-based ICBMs, that exceeded what most U.S. intelligence analysts believed it would do. As a result, by the mid-1970s U.S. intelligence was being accused by some of having underestimated the Soviet threat. Some critics argued along ideological grounds that the U.S. Intelligence Community never truly understood the fears and anxieties that drove Soviet defense planning and decisions.

WINDOW OF VULNERABILITY

By the mid-1970s there were a number of experts, both inside and outside the U.S. government, who believed that advances in Soviet strategic nuclear force deployments and developments had created a "window of vulnerability" for the United States and its Allies. This led to the President's Foreign Intelligence Advisory Board calling on then Director of Central Intelligence and the CIA George H. W. Bush to invite outside experts to critique the Intelligence Community's annual NIE on Soviet strategic nuclear forces—the so-called A/B Team competition. Unfortunately, this exercise was politically motivated and turned out to be less an objective critique than an ideological one.

Nevertheless, as noted by former DCI and CIA director Robert Gates in his book *From the Shadows: The Ultimate Insider's Story of Five Presidents and How They Won the Cold War*, the Soviets had in fact poured enormous, albeit scarce, resources into a huge buildup of their strategic nuclear offensive forces following their Cuban gambit in 1962. It had taken the Intelligence Community some time to recognize that the Soviets were not just going for parity but, in the view of some experts, for superiority. Thus, there were allegations that the Intelligence Community had underestimated Soviet capabilities and that, by the early 1980s, U.S. strategic nuclear forces would be vulnerable to a first-strike attack. In 1976 and subsequent years, the Intelligence Community called increased attention to the strides the Soviets were making, both numerically and qualitatively.

Despite the many accusations that the Intelligence Community consistently underestimated Soviet nuclear capabilities and intentions, the record indicates that there was no systematic bias in the NIEs; at times the Intelligence Community had overestimated Soviet capabilities, as during the missile gap crisis of the late 1950s, and other times had underestimated them, as during the mid-1970s.[19] The underestimates were usually associated with the numbers of missiles and warheads deployed, while the overestimates tended to be on the side of attributing to the Soviets greater technical advances than they had actually made. In any case, these inaccurate estimates were largely attributable to a lack of good data or a lag in our appreciation for what the Soviets were doing or would choose to do in various situations. This, in turn, drove the Intelligence Community to devise more sophisticated means of understanding Soviet force developments and intentions. Ultimately, the advances made contributed to the ability of the United States to more accurately monitor military activity and to more reliably verify arms control treaties with the Soviet Union.

4

Strategic Arms Control Legitimizes
Space-Based Reconnaissance

BY THE MID-1960S the nuclear arms race was becoming ever more

intense. The United States was constructing a thousand under-

ground launch silos for its new Minuteman ICBM, capable on very

short notice of delivering nuclear weapons to Soviet territory in less

than thirty minutes with considerable accuracy. The Soviet Union

was deploying hundreds of ICBMs itself, and by the 1970s was threat-

ening to exceed the U.S. total. Soviet ICBMs were less accurate than the U.S. Minuteman, but the larger nuclear warheads deployed with their missiles had significantly greater explosive yields. Indeed, the Soviet SS-9 ICBM carried a 25–megaton nuclear warhead, in contrast to the largest warhead yield of about 1 megaton on the new U.S. Minuteman missiles. However, in the 1970s both the United States and the Soviet Union began to deploy MIRVed warheads, which had smaller yields—in the hundreds of kilotons. Because the newer missiles were more accurate and the warheads considerably more numerous, these MIRVed warheads could achieve the same, indeed greater, destructive potential as single, large but less accurate warheads.[1]

Both sides were also planning the development and deployment of antimissile missiles, or antiballistic missile systems (ABMs). The advent of this technology threatened to exacerbate the arms race in two ways. First, it undermined deterrence theory in that if country A were to build an ABM defense, country B might fear that once the defense was in place, country A could carry out a first nuclear strike against the strategic forces (ICBMs, submarine-launched missiles, and long-range bombers) of country B and use its ABM defense to ward off the substantially weakened retaliatory attack by country B. Country A could thus win a nuclear war. As a result, if country B perceives that the ABM defenses of country A are superior to its own, it may decide that it had better be sure to strike first in a crisis. Thus, crisis stability, which is maintained by a roughly equal balance of strategic forces, is undermined. Second, arms race stability is undercut as well in that if one side builds more ICBMs to overcome the ABMs of the other side, then the second side likely would conclude that it needs more ICBMs and perhaps should add to its ABM deployments, and so it goes.

Without question something needed to be done or the nuclear arms race would get completely out of hand. In 1967 President Lyndon Johnson raised with Soviet Premier Alexei Kosygin at the Glassboro, New Jersey, Summit meeting the possibility of limiting ABM deployments. In 1968 the United States and the Soviet Union agreed to begin negotiations on both offensive (missiles and bombers) and defensive

(ABMs) strategic nuclear systems. However, the agreement was derailed by the Soviet invasion of Czechoslovakia in August 1968. Only after President Nixon took office did the SALT negotiations formally begin in Helsinki, Finland, in November 1969. As one participant in the negotiations stated,

There are a number of considerations which have brought the two countries to the conference table to discuss strategic arms limitation. Among the most important are: first, the emergence on each side of a perception of mutual deterrence and rough strategic parity; secondly, an awareness on each side that another round in the arms race, while costly in terms of human and material resources, would almost certainly not bring greater security to either country; and third, the availability on each side of intelligence collection systems capable of monitoring the military programs of the other country without infringing on its territory. The development in intelligence techniques and capabilities, required by the imperatives of the race in strategic armaments, have helped create the conditions in which the two sides can move toward verifiable limitations on such armaments.[2]

The objectives of the SALT negotiations were further refined in an exchange of letters in 1971 between President Nixon and Soviet General Secretary Brezhnev, which called for a treaty limiting strategic defensive systems and the first-ever interim limits on strategic offensive systems. It seemed that the modest steps taken to cap strategic offensive nuclear forces were accepted by the Soviets as the price required to stop the U.S. ABM buildup. However, it was not clear that either side was as yet willing to consider more comprehensive constraints on their offensive nuclear forces.

But to reach even these modest objectives, the agreed-upon constraints had to be effectively (i.e., independently and reliably) verifiable, especially in the view of the United States. Given Soviet secrecy and Cold War suspicions, along with the history of false starts because of inadequate verification, the only way this could happen would be by means of national technical sources and methods, including the use of reconnaissance satellite systems, which by now were being deployed by both sides. Largely to mask that these monitoring capabilities were in fact national intelligence capabilities, both sides adopted the euphemism "national technical means of verification."

Guided largely by the achievements in overhead reconnaissance, efforts to control the nuclear arms race in the latter part of the 1960s

NATIONAL TECHNICAL MEANS OF VERIFICATION

By the late 1960s, both the United States and the Soviet Union had developed remote technical collection systems to monitor the military activities of each other, as well as other selected countries. In addition, they had created analytic processes and procedures by which they interpreted and analyzed the data from the collection systems. Together these capabilities are referred to in the intelligence world as sensitive sources and methods, which include all efforts to collect and analyze data on foreign adversaries, particularly potential military threats.

Many people believe that remote technical collection is limited to photographic satellites, given that such satellites are best known and are designed to circle the globe and to collect information on otherwise denied areas. To be sure, these systems include reconnaissance satellites of various types, but they also include other important capabilities such as aerial, sea-based, and ground-based collectors. The products of these collection efforts include photographs, electronic signals such as frequencies from radars, telemetry signals from aircraft and missile tests, communications intercepts, seismic data, and radionuclide samples from nuclear test explosions. The exact details of such systems are largely classified to ensure their continued effectiveness and protection against efforts to spoof them.

Because neither the United States nor the Soviet Union wanted to advertise or even admit to the use of intelligence sources and methods to verify arms control treaties, both eventually agreed to use the phrase "national technical means of verification," or NTM, which left it ambiguous and up to each side to determine which intelligence sources and methods were most appropriate to use for the monitoring tasks at hand. Those tasks differed, as one would expect, depending on whether the monitoring targets were ground, naval, air, conventional, or nuclear forces. To be sure, U.S. intelligence monitoring capabilities were carefully explained to executive branch policy makers as well as to members of Congress during closed congressional ratification hearings, but there was almost no public discussion of U.S. NTM capabilities and certainly no public discussion by the Soviets regarding their systems.

The only time NTM capabilities have been openly criticized and discussed in an international forum was during the negotiation of the CTBT in the mid-1990s. The United States, Russian Federation, United Kingdom, France, and a few other countries favored the treaty's making explicit the right to use NTM to monitor nuclear explosions. The countries most opposed, especially China, India, and Pakistan, tried to get the United States and Russia to define what they meant by NTM. Both refused, arguing that any definition would facilitate cheating and unnecessarily restrict future developments of collection systems, which would be unwise in the context of an indefinite treaty. They did provide examples, such as space, aerial, sea-, and ground-based detectors, as well as nationally owned and operated systems that paralleled those planned for the CTBT's International Monitoring System.

focused on limiting ground-based missile launchers and silos, submarines, and nuclear weapon delivery vehicles such as missiles and bombers—items large enough to be counted and analyzed through the use of reconnaissance satellites and other technical intelligence capabilities. Such capabilities were also critical to monitoring the large Warsaw Pact conventional forces located in Eastern Europe and the western Soviet Union. Understanding their numbers, training maneuvers, and capabilities was critical to NATO war planning. In the agreements themselves these systems were, as mentioned, euphemistically referred to as NTM (the term has survived to the present). Neither side favored publicly acknowledging or enshrining in a treaty text the use of its intelligence capabilities to monitor treaty-relevant activities.

With the agreement on the nomenclature of NTM, the treaty limiting ABM systems (ABM Treaty) and the Interim Agreement on Strategic Offensive Arms could be completed. The two agreements were signed by President Nixon and General Secretary Brezhnev on May 26, 1972, in Moscow. They became what is referred to as the SALT I agreements. The ABM Treaty limited each side to two ABM deployments (later reduced to one), and the Interim Agreement more or less froze the deployments of land-based and submarine-launched strategic missile systems as they were in 1972. This was a landmark achievement, providing the first limits on the nuclear arms race and agreed means of verification after the two agreements entered into force in October of that year. All subsequent agreements limiting nuclear weapons owe a debt to these first SALT agreements. When asked in 1972 how many ICBMs the Soviets would have built had the SALT I agreements not been in place, a Soviet official said, "Until our Generals said that we had enough."[3]

Legitimizing Space-Based Reconnaissance

But these agreements would not have been possible if they had not been designed to be verifiable primarily by the early reconnaissance satellites of the two sides. These systems could image the ground-based missile launchers and ballistic missile submarines of the two sides. And as mentioned above, the limits of the two agreements were on ground-based missile launchers and submarines capable of launching missiles (as well as on radars in the case of the ABM Treaty)—items large enough to be detected by satellites and counted by analysts. Launchers rather than missile inventories were considered the appropriate item to limit in that, in 1972, launchers were not viewed as being sufficiently rapidly reloadable (i.e., they could not effectively launch more than one missile without considerable refurbishment between launchings) to alter the strategic balance codified in the treaty.

Thus, the international legal legitimacy of using national technical intelligence collection and analytic sources and methods was carefully enshrined in both agreements, in contrast to Khrushchev's earlier complaints about satellite espionage. (See Appendix B for details of the SALT I agreements.) After the launch of Sputnik, French president de Gaulle had reportedly chided Khrushchev about the fact that a Soviet satellite was passing over Paris multiple times per day. Khrushchev is reported to have replied that anyone might take all the pictures he wished from satellites over Soviet territory. Given this attitude, the United States, and subsequently other countries, concluded that reconnaissance by satellites was not an issue that would be seriously challenged internationally on the basis of trespassing territorial air space, as had been the case with reconnaissance aircraft.[4]

NTM Provisions

Article XII of the ABM Treaty and Article VI of the Interim Agreement provide that the provisions of the treaties shall be verified by national technical means "operating in accordance with generally accepted principles of international law." This means two very important things: First, reconnaissance satellites are legal under international law and therefore appropriate vehicles by which to verify arms control agreements. Second, aircraft overflights (meaning by U-2–type aircraft) are not. As a result, no aircraft overflights would be permitted to verify the SALT I agreements; only orbiting reconnaissance satellites were legitimized. Thus, the creation of these systems and their formal recognition by the United States and the Soviet Union made possible the first agreements limiting nuclear weapons in spite of the hostile atmosphere of the Cold War.

But this was not all. The two parties also agreed to protect the right of NTM verification in the treaty text. The second paragraph of this verification article provides that neither party shall interfere with NTM recognized by the treaty, and the third paragraph provides that neither party shall engage in deliberate concealment practices that could frustrate NTM. The second paragraph is clear: NTM is to be protected from obstructive measures such as blinding with lasers or electronic jamming. The understandings about the third paragraph have undergone many changes over the years. In the first instance it was designed simply to prohibit things such as covering silo launcher facilities with canvas or camouflage or the like. Later it came to mean access to missile test signals or telemetry, and gradually it evolved into a synonym for active cooperation in verification. And while imagery—photography—was generally accepted as the ultimate proof of a violation, these other verification technologies were important to protect. For example, the Soviet SA-5 missile was excluded finally from consideration as an ABM interceptor during the SALT I negotiations due to data collected from telemetry, radar measurements, and communications intercepts, all of which showed that this system did not have real ABM capabilities.

These provisions enshrining the legality and protection for satellite reconnaissance systems in the first SALT agreements were considered by many at the time and subsequently to be the most important provisions of the agreements. They made it possible to take the first steps in nuclear weapons arms control, and they opened the door to much of the progress since. Variations on these provisions are found in almost every subsequent arms control agreement, even into the post–Cold War era. In addition, confidence-building measures, data exchanges, and on-site inspections were subsequently added to NTM provisions to create a more robust verification regime.

Nevertheless, nothing was said publicly about the characteristics and capabilities of NTM for nearly a decade. It was only in 1978, as a prelude to the ratification proceedings for SALT II, that President Carter, after a long internal U.S. government struggle, officially disclosed the role of intelligence collection systems in monitoring treaties.[5] Although two decades earlier Eisenhower had been advised to make the fact of satellite reconnaissance public, he decided that this would put the United States on a slippery slope of having to divulge more details than would be in the U.S. national interest.[6] The Soviet Union was not the only country of intelligence interest, and other countries would likely object to public disclosures of remote intelligence collection efforts. Some activities were better left unmentioned. Also, by not disclosing publicly the fact of satellite reconnaissance and using the term NTM, it was easier to bypass potential legal challenges to such systems.

Ratification Hearings

During the SALT I congressional approval process, the lack of data on the Soviet systems limited by the agreements became an issue that impacted all subsequent bilateral negotiations with the Soviets. At a hearing before the Senate Armed Services Committee in July 1972, with members of the U.S. SALT I delegation as the testifying witnesses, Senator Henry Jackson of Washington pressed with some vigor on the lack of agreed-upon data on Soviet systems. The U.S. chief negotiator, Ambassador Gerard Smith, explained that agreement on the number of Soviet ICBM launchers existing at the time of the signing of the SALT I Interim Agreement was not needed to determine whether there had been any violation of the freeze on their number imposed by the agreement; the U.S. government knew perfectly well how many there were. Senator Jackson responded in effect that this was not good enough: the U.S. government knows how many Soviet ICBM launchers there are; he, Senator Jackson, knows and (pointing to a Soviet embassy representative in the audience) there is a representative of the Soviet Union in the audience who knows; but the American people do not know, and this is unacceptable.[7]

The issue lingered on during the SALT I hearings. As a result, achieving an agreed-upon database became a major U.S. negotiating objective in the SALT II and subsequent negotiations. This led to the vast data exchanges of the Intermediate-Range Nuclear Forces Treaty of 1987, the Conventional Armed Forces in Europe Treaty of 1990, and the Strategic Offensive Arms Reduction Treaty of 1991. All of this contributed to enhancing the effectiveness of NTM monitoring and, therefore, confidence in verification of the treaty.

U.S. NTM Capabilities

The United States possesses, as do a few other countries, an impressive array of technical collection systems, many of which are used for arms control monitoring, depending on the treaty. The United States has devoted considerable effort to improving its intelligence collection and analytic capabilities, often in response to congressional pressure, to be better prepared to monitor arms control agreements under almost all conditions.

Some of the imagery satellites have been designed for area surveillance (i.e., to cover a wide area for detecting significant activities), while others have been equipped with higher-resolution cameras permitting them to detect small, technical details but over a much smaller area. In addition, satellite-based radars can penetrate cloud cover and monitor in darkness, unlike the optical sensors that are dependent upon daylight and good weather. Such systems permit intelligence analysts to cover a wide variety of targets on a regular basis, which makes it possible for them to follow developments as they occur (see Appendix C for more details on U.S. reconnaissance systems).

Large ground-based and ship-borne radars, cameras, and infrared sensors complement satellites by making it possible to monitor aircraft and missile flights as well as the reentry of missile warheads. These sensors are generally directed at monitoring qualitative characteristics of aircraft and missiles to determine their capabilities and compliance with treaty provisions. This is in contrast to imagery satellites, which are more suitable for tracking the quantitative aspects of force development and treaty compliance.

Electronic surveillance is also critical for monitoring certain provisions of some treaties, especially when dealing with issues such as the transmission of telemetry from the test flights of aircraft and missiles, as was negotiated under the SALT II treaty. Passive receivers located in space, on aircraft, ships, and ground vehicles can pick up various electronic transmissions from communications, radars, and military equipment of various types.

Seismic, hydroacoustic, infrasound, and radionuclide monitoring sensors are used on various collection platforms to detect nuclear explosions. Given that such explosions normally create shockwaves and at times disperse radioactive debris and gases into the atmosphere, there is now a worldwide network of detectors focused on these events. Some of these national sensors also contribute to the CTBT's International Monitoring System, but many more are nationally owned and operated.

Despite impressive technical capabilities, NTM systems are neither foolproof nor omnipresent. Weather and darkness can inhibit imagery systems, unless they also include radar and infrared systems, and orbiting satellites and aircraft are not able to remain over a target of interest indefinitely. Target countries can take advantage of these weaknesses by planning their sensitive activity during those periods when collections systems may not be in view. Or, as in the case of telemetry, countries can choose to hide their data through encryption or encapsulation (i.e., recording but not transmitting data during flight). In the case of nuclear testing, it is possible to hide small yields, given that technology is not yet available to monitor with complete confidence down to zero yield, especially if evasive measures are used.

Because of these challenges, countries typically use redundant and complementary systems as part of their NTM architecture in a synergistic manner to maximize confidence that suspicious activity will be detected before it becomes strategically significant. And to enhance their monitoring capabilities, the parties strive to include treaty provisions designed to maximize the capabilities of their NTM systems and to prevent interference with legitimate monitoring activities.

Monitoring Quantitative vs. Qualitative Provisions

When examining the challenge of verifying strategic nuclear force treaties, negotiators have had to keep in mind that there are multiple monitoring tasks involved. The most basic item of accountability is the number of launchers and launch platforms (i.e., missile silos, land-based mobile launchers, ABM launchers, submarines, and bombers) as well as delivery vehicles (i.e., missiles). Such items are used to determine force size and location, and they typically become the "units of account" when determining whether a side is in compliance with the basic obligations of a treaty. However, the more sophisticated and comprehensive treaties also contain restrictions on qualitative aspects of the forces, such as types and sizes of missiles, submarines, and bombers as well as weapon ranges and payload capabilities.

These distinguishing characteristics are often determined during the flight testing of the systems. Some characteristics can be determined through satellite imagery, others require electronic test data. This is where telemetry plays a major role. The performance signals from test flights are transmitted to their designers so that subsystems can be monitored and problems identified if there is a failure. If each party to an agreement can intercept and read those signals, each can have increased confidence that the other party is not developing or deploying a system that is restricted or banned by the treaty.

It is easy to see that military officials are as interested in such weapon system characteristics for planning operations as are those responsible for monitoring or verifying another country's forces under a treaty. That is why during the major internal U.S. debate on Soviet telemetry encryption practices during the endgame of SALT II, the Director of Central Intelligence and the Secretary of Defense took particularly hard positions requiring treaty language prohibiting the encryption of telemetry on treaty-limited weapons systems. This set the stage for a major issue involving telemetry monitoring as the SALT II negotiations neared conclusion (see chapter 6 for details). Also, in eventually concluding that the Soviet Backfire bomber did not have the range to be included as a heavy bomber within the definition in the SALT II treaty, the United States decided that only the collection and analysis of telemetry and other signals would provide sufficient data for verification; photographs alone could not settle the issue of range.

5

Intelligence Support to Arms Control Activities

THE U.S. INTELLIGENCE COMMUNITY, though not an advocate or

defender of policy, is an intimate and critical contributor to U.S.

national security deliberations and planning. Intelligence informa-

tion and analysis regarding the capabilities and intentions of foreign

strategic threats provide the baseline understanding for defense and

national security policy planning. Through the interagency process

in Washington, to which intelligence officials contribute raw reports, written analyses, and briefings, the Intelligence Community constantly provides policy makers with the best information and understanding it can so that well-informed policy decisions can be made.

Information

In terms of intelligence support to arms control initiatives, the Intelligence Community provides information at various stages of the process. First, intelligence provides insights into what a foreign country's military programs and capabilities are as well as what its negotiating objectives are likely to be, including what they want from the United States as well as what they are likely to be willing to give up in the negotiation. To obtain the information required to produce such insights requires that the Intelligence Community utilize smart and clever approaches. It also requires that policy makers make clear what their policy needs and priorities are for intelligence collection and analysis. Moreover, the Intelligence Community helps policy makers determine what sort of verification provisions would be desirable, should there be a treaty, to complement our own NTM capabilities and to optimize our ability to monitor activities and ensure credible and effective verification.

The late former Director of Central Intelligence Richard Helms focused on intelligence support to arms control during an address to the National War College in October 1971. According to his now declassified address, he stated that

since 1969, it [intelligence support to the SALT negotiations] has grown so rapidly in importance and urgency that it now is one of our foremost continuing concerns. Intelligence has major roles to play. We are responsible for defining the Soviet strategic capabilities which are to be limited in any treaty. After any agreement is signed, we will be even more involved in continually monitoring whether the Soviets are observing those limits. An agreement as wide-ranging as the one contemplated at SALT has had to await the advent of a reliable, repeatable means of verification from outside the USSR. This brings me into an area in which I must tread with the greatest care. I am talking, of course, about satellite reconnaissance. Everyone knows that this activity is going on. And yet we go to considerable lengths—and endure considerable inconvenience—to maintain a security barrier around it. There are two excellent reasons for this. One is that certain details of the program still must be kept from the Soviets if it is to remain fully effective. The second is that the Soviets themselves are very anxious that it not be discussed. They are aware of what we are doing, although not of the extent of our success, and they have a vigorous program of their own. In fact, last year they launched about three times as many reconnaissance satellites as we did.

If a treaty is finally achieved, you will find this point covered in language like 'national technical means of verification, operating within the generally accepted principles of international law.' There will be no misunderstanding between Washington and Moscow about what is meant. But we'll avoid a lot of problems by saying it that way. The first full-system success came in 1960, almost overlapping with the last U-2 flight over Soviet territory. Since then, reliability has become excellent. The performance of the system, as well as the quality of the product, has dramatically improved. It has come to embrace electronic, infrared, and other kinds of intelligence in addition to imagery. We have reached the point where we can give to the President some definite assurances about just what sort of treaty provisions we can and cannot monitor with confidence.'[1]

Expertise

Second, during the actual negotiations, intelligence officials continually update policy makers, both those conducting the negotiation and those reviewing policy in Washington, on any significant developments that might affect the direction and outcome of the negotiations. During the SALT I negotiations, it was decided to make intelligence officers available to support the delegations. Analysts with technical and strategic force backgrounds were deemed to possess the appropriate knowledge and expertise, and they were backstopped by groups of similar analysts in Washington as well as the experts responsible for collection systems. As advisers to the delegations, they reported on the latest intelligence information and analysis, responded to requests for additional intelligence information, provided advice on specific treaty language and provisions, helped prepare formal delegation statements, and contributed to analyses of the negotiations for messages back to Washington. As is the case in Washington where the Intelligence Community supports National Security Council deliberations, intelligence advisers on the delegations do not make or recommend policy but rather provide objective analyses of the facts, representing Intelligence Community–wide perspectives.[2]

During the SALT I negotiations and a considerable portion of the SALT II negotiations, the Intelligence Community was represented by the late Howard Stoertz, who at the same time served as the National Intelligence Officer for Strategic Programs (i.e., strategic nuclear forces) and was therefore of high rank. He was assisted by an able team of experts on the delegation backed up by others in Washington. The Washington-based staff had begun in the early 1970s with about six people but grew to almost a hundred by the early 1990s.

Stoertz's expertise on Soviet strategic nuclear forces made him an indispensable member of the U.S. delegation. As a full member of the negotiating team, he served under the auspices of the Department of State and was so listed on the U.S. delegation. This fooled no one, including the Soviets, but it kept up appearances. Everyone knew who was who on both delegations. When Stoertz left the U.S. delegation after nearly seven years, Colonel Norman Clyne, the chief of staff of the U.S. delegation, informed his counterpart on the Soviet delegation, Vadim Chulitsky, that the U.S. delegation would have a new member, Mr. John Whitman. "What agency is he from?" asked Chulitsky. Clyne responded, "the State Department." "And whom is he replacing?" responded Chulitsky. "Mr. Howard Stoertz," Clyne replied. "Oh, that wing of the State Department," Chulitsky replied.

On another occasion a very unpleasant man representing the KGB joined the Soviet delegation. The word was that he was a ruthless official who years before had interrogated an American aircrew flying an RB-47 aircraft over the northwestern border of the Soviet Union on a reconnaissance mission. The plane was shot down by Soviet fighters and the crew was captured after it crash-landed. There were reports that the crew had been treated roughly by the Soviet interrogators led by this particular individual. The KGB official, although Russian and Soviet, had an Irish name. A brilliant Russian linguist on the American side, who always enjoyed good rapport with his Soviet military counterparts, let drop with one of the Soviets that the United States understood that this KGB official was the son of Irish revolutionaries who had emigrated to the Soviet Union years ago. And wasn't that interesting? The official was recalled to Moscow in three days, and occasionally there were thankful hints from Soviet delegates.

Congressional Testimony

Third, intelligence officials are called upon also to provide expert testimony regarding any treaty that is sent to the Senate for its advice and consent. Traditionally, the Director of Central Intelligence, now presumably the new Director of National Intelligence, testifies on the ability of the U.S. Intelligence Community to monitor the relevant activities of the other party or parties to the agreement. Such testimonies cover the capabilities of NTM to monitor specific provisions of the treaty in question as well as the synergy between NTM and the various verification provisions included in the particular treaty.

This emphasis on intelligence monitoring, vice verification, is quite intentional within the U.S. government. Only U.S. policy officials (ultimately the President), not intelligence officials, have the responsibility to charge that a particular action by another country is in violation of an international agreement. The role of U.S. intelligence is to understand and report on what other countries are doing under any given treaty. This division of labor evolved largely because of the great international political impact of accusing another country of cheating. It also was a means to keep U.S. intelligence from becoming politicized.

Accordingly, formal Intelligence Community testimony on its monitoring capabilities with regard to any treaty is intended to inform decision makers, not make judgments regarding a country's compliance. Verification, therefore, is a political judgment, not a technical or intelligence one. The administration must decide what to do in response to information provided by the Intelligence Community. Declaring whether a party to a treaty is or is not in compliance with its obligations under a treaty is politically sensitive.

In addition to testimony from intelligence officials, ratification hearings normally include testimony from the departments of Defense, State, and possibly Energy in the case of a nuclear treaty. It is the responsibility of Defense to report on the effect of the agreement on U.S. force capabilities and to determine whether any potential cheating would be significant enough to constitute a military threat to our national security interests. And it is the responsibility of State to convince the Senate that the United States is better off with than without the treaty and that it is, on balance, verifiable.

Continuous Monitoring

After a treaty enters into force, the Intelligence Community's monitoring responsibility continues for the duration of the agreement, and it is intimately involved in any subsequent deliberations over compliance issues. Given that NTM is likely to be the means by which the United States detects activities of concern, intelligence officials are called upon both to report on and to explain any suspicious activities detected. During the Cold War, no issue was more contentious and politically charged than that of Soviet compliance with existing arms control agreements. And the question of compliance goes to the heart of arms control monitoring. Congress demands and receives periodic compliance reports from the executive branch. For example, during the years 1984, 1985, and 1986, the House conducted hearings on Soviet "likely," "probable," or "potential" violations of nine arms control treaty provisions. Testimony was given by both policy and intelligence agencies.[3]

One of the issues that was raised concerned continued Soviet encryption practices, which appeared to violate the SALT II ban on encrypting telemetry, an activity that impeded verification. The House Permanent Select Committee on Intelligence concluded that the treaty language had failed to establish unambiguous and firm standards for determining compliance with this obligation, which intelligence officials had warned would be the case. The majority of expert witnesses concluded that, rather than a clear violation, the Soviet practices under the treaty had exploited an inherently flawed provision. Such encryption made it difficult for the Intelligence Community using its NTM to assess treaty-relevant missile performance characteristics, but it had not totally prevented intelligence analysts from estimating key parameters.[4] Also in the early 1980s, U.S. NTM detected the construction of a large phased-array radar in a location that proved to be in violation of the ABM Treaty. After political consideration, this issue was raised with the Soviets, who initially tried to mask the radar's function but ultimately acknowledged their "mistake" and agreed to dismantle the radar.[5]

This, along with a number of other incidents during the Cold War, demonstrated that U.S. intelligence is continuously under the gun to detect and explain activities that are of compliance concern. The Intelligence Community must not only evaluate its ability to monitor provisions that are advocated by the policy community during the negotiations by clearly articulating the extent of its analytic uncertainties, but it also must actively assess potential cheating scenarios so that both the administration and Congress can be confident that all avenues of significant circumvention are appropriately and comprehensively addressed in future agreements.

Protecting NTM Capabilities against Compromise and Interference

The flip side of using unique and sophisticated intelligence collection and analytic capabilities both to monitor Soviet strategic developments as well as support arms control initiatives is the requirement to protect the specific capabilities of those NTM systems and at times even their existence. To the extent the Soviets were able to gain access to information on the systems, they likely were able to develop ways to thwart their effective use. Thus, elaborate measures were established, including cover stories such as "Discoverer" in the case of the Corona program, to protect this fragile capability to monitor Soviet strategic force activities. As stated earlier, it was only in the late 1970s that the United States officially acknowledged that it uses satellite reconnaissance systems to monitor compliance with arms control treaties.

As would be expected, during the Cold War the Soviet Union devoted considerable energy and effort to obtaining information about U.S. intelligence collection systems and programs, including those dedicated to monitoring compliance with arms control treaties. Unfortunately, on several occasions aspects of these capabilities were compromised. For example, the United States developed and deployed satellites of the Rhyolite type into high orbits that allowed them to hover over specific areas collecting SIGINT (signals intelligence, meaning communications and other electronic emissions from weapons systems), which provided Washington a flood of data about Soviet military capabilities and leadership communications. This was particularly useful in monitoring the development of new missile systems. But in the mid-1970s the secrets of the system were sold to the Russians by one of the employees of the company that had built the satellite system and helped operate it. This security breach by the Boyce/Lee espionage ring led to increased Soviet encryption of their most sensitive military communications and to a major issue regarding telemetry encryption during the SALT II negotiations.[6] In the same timeframe, a disgruntled CIA employee sold the top secret operational manual for the new KH-11 electro-optical imaging satellite to the Soviets, which provided them the information they needed to take evasive measures against the system.[7]

Thus, within a few years, two state-of-the-art intelligence collection systems, which were essential both to understanding Soviet military capabilities and monitoring Soviet activities under arms control agreements, had been compromised. These losses were detrimental to U.S. ability to monitor Soviet activities under contemporary arms control agreements, and the Intelligence Community had to seek alternative means to support robust verification.

The threat to NTM satellite reconnaissance systems also came from U.S.-Soviet rivalry in space. Despite the provisions included in their bilateral agreements designed to protect the effectiveness of verification through national technical means, both countries explored anti-satellite (ASAT) weapons systems. The concept was to blind the other side and interrupt its military communications during any nuclear conflict by destroying its space-based reconnaissance and communications capabilities. Such ASAT weapons could be direct-ascent, ground-launched missiles; orbiting space-based weapons that could target other space objects; or ground-based lasers. The Soviet Union was credited with having the only operational nonnuclear ASAT system, a ground-based interceptor that could place in space a co-orbital satellite designed to collide with the satellite that was being attacked.[8]

At one point in the late 1970s, the United States and Soviet Union engaged in ASAT negotiations to determine what, if anything, they might do to regulate such capabilities, which were potentially destabilizing. It appears that both sides recognized that ensuring the operational integrity of their respective space-based NTM systems was critical to their efforts to forge a stable strategic relationship. This required that they back away from ASAT capabilities. President Reagan's proposal of 1983 for a space-based missile defense, the subsequent U.S. Strategic Defense Initiative program, and contemporary discussions of using space for weapon programs all raise concerns regarding the ultimate survivability of space-based reconnaissance systems in a crisis when NTM-type capabilities are exactly what countries need to prevent crises from getting out of hand.

As was mentioned earlier, both sides recognized the need to protect the effectiveness of their NTM monitoring capabilities to enhance the verifiability of the treaties being negotiated. Thus, they added language in the verification provisions that required measures to be taken so as not to interfere with monitoring systems and activities. These included prohibitions against concealment measures. As confidence and trust grew between the two sides, they also agreed to include provisions that required the exchange of databases on their force size and locations as well as cooperative measures designed to enhance the capability of their respective NTM systems to monitor treaty-limited activities. Ultimately, this included ensuring the transmission of electronic test data without masking them during the flight tests of missiles and aircraft during their development or as part of exercises.

6

National Technical Means of Verification
Takes Center Stage

AS INDICATED in the previous chapter, the United States possesses

a variety of technical intelligence means, both active and passive, to

support arms control activities under almost all weather and light-

ing conditions. The principal U.S. NTM instruments are recon-

naissance satellite systems using photographic, infrared, radar, and

electronic sensors; ground-based radars, seismic and communica-

tions collection stations; sea-based sensors; and underwater acoustic systems. These systems often supplement and overlap each other, making it possible to use the synergy among them to cross-check data for accuracy. Depending on the treaty provision being monitored, one or more of the capabilities takes the lead while the others comple- ment and provide support.

The Challenge of Monitoring Strategic Arms Control Treaties

Despite the acceptance in the 1970s of NTM by the United States and the Soviet Union in the SALT agreements, and subsequently by the rest of the world, albeit reluctantly, in other agreements, as legit- imate verification tools, skeptics have tended to question the verifica- tion claims of those who support various treaties. In contrast to SALT I, where U.S. NTM capabilities and monitoring judgments were gen- erally accepted with relatively little debate, the SALT II negotiations and subsequent ratification hearings focused heavily on U.S. capabili- ties to monitor the activities of Soviet strategic nuclear forces under quite detailed conditions. In comparison to SALT I, the SALT II treaty was comprehensive in its limitations and restrictions, which increased the monitoring and verification challenge. Despite strong testimony that the SALT II treaty of 1979 was effectively verifiable using NTM alone, the treaty's verifiability was questioned by some senators dur- ing the ratification hearings in the summer of 1979. Senator John Glenn, a prominent Democratic member of the Senate Foreign Rela- tions Committee, led the way.

Senator Glenn, who had made informal visits to the SALT I nego- tiations in the early 1970s, visited the SALT II negotiations in Geneva in the summer of 1977 as an official Senate observer. Secretary of State Cyrus Vance had requested the appointment of congressional observers to the U.S. SALT delegation pursuant to a suggestion by then Director of the Arms Control and Disarmament Agency Paul Warnke. Congress responded by appointing observers from each house, thereby establishing a principle that continued through the Strategic Arms Reduction Treaty (START) negotiations of the 1980s and early 1990s. Many members of Congress visited the U.S. SALT II delegation between 1977 and 1979, when the negotiations were concluded. The Senate, as the eventual ratifying body, was somewhat more active than the House, although many House members visited as well. It was arranged that members of Congress who were officially designated observers by Congress were temporarily appointed to the U.S. delegation as participants in the negotiating process. In this role they attended formal plenary meetings and were always given a private meeting with the Soviet chief negotiator accompanied by the U.S. delegation head.

In these visits by members of Congress, verification was always one of the principal issues discussed with the Soviets. Most senators, usually well briefed by the intelligence representatives on the U.S. delegation as to U.S. NTM capabilities, were satisfied that the emerging SALT II treaty would be fully verifiable. In other words, that NTM would make the treaty "adequately verifiable" (later "effectively verifiable"), to use the code word of the day.[1] Everyone recognized that 100 percent verification could not be achieved. In addition, in order to assist NTM, various type rules and cooperative measures were developed in the course of the negotiations. However, neither party had yet reached the point where it was willing to include intrusive, on-site inspections as part of the treaty's verification regime.

Counting Rules

Treaty language established limits and definitions that made possible verification through NTM even without direct observation. For example, since NTM could not actually count the number of nuclear warheads on a specific ICBM deployed in a silo, it was agreed that an ICBM of a particular type (e.g., Minuteman, SS-18, SS-19) would be credited with the maximum number of warheads with which it had ever been tested. This was verifiable by NTM. Second, since it was difficult for NTM to determine what type of missile actually was deployed in a given ICBM silo launcher (the silos were largely underground and their doors on the surface were usually closed), a type rule was developed for this as well. It provided that if a missile with MIRVs had ever been associated with a silo launcher of a particular type, all launchers of that type would be considered launchers of MIRVed missiles and counted under the relevant treaty limit. Similar arrangements were agreed upon to cover missiles carried by submarines.

This second rule not only enhanced verification but it also affected Soviet strategic deployments. For example, at the Derazhnaya and Pervomaisk missile sites in Ukraine, there were 180 silo launchers of a type that at least on one occasion had been associated with the deployment of the Soviet SS-19 missile, which had been tested with MIRVs. U.S. intelligence sources were aware that the Soviets had deployed the single-warhead SS-11 ICBM in these silo launchers. Nevertheless, the U.S. delegation insisted that these 180 silo launchers count as launchers of MIRVed ICBMs (on which the SALT II treaty placed a limit of 820), even though in fact single-warhead missiles were deployed therein, because this type of launcher had once been associated with the SS-19. The Soviet delegation violently protested for more than a year that this was unfair, but the U.S. delegation stuck firmly to the type rule. Finally, in the closing months of the negotiations, in the spring of 1979, the Soviets conceded. Subsequently, the Soviet ambassador told the U.S. ambassador that the delegation had agreed with the U.S. position from the start but that it had taken a year of argument by cable with the bureaucrats in Moscow to convince their authorities that these NTM type rules were important to the Soviet side as well and that the Americans were correct on this point.[2]

Database Exchanges

As previously stated, using NTM, assisted by the two type rules, to verify the number of weapons systems that made up the strategic forces on each side (e.g., the total number of ICBM silo launchers,

MIRVed ICBM silo launchers, ballistic missile submarines, heavy bombers, etc.) was quite feasible. Nevertheless, the United States wanted this confirmed by both sides in an agreed-upon one-page statement of data. As mentioned in chapter 4, the lack of such a statement of data had been a serious political liability in the SALT I Senate ratification hearings. The U.S. delegation was determined not to repeat this mistake in SALT II. However, this new U.S. requirement was anathema to the Soviets. It was acceptable to the Soviets that the United States would gain this knowledge through the operation of NTM, but to agree to these numbers in a public treaty document was quite another thing indeed. Upon visiting Geneva, many senators stressed to the Soviets the importance of an agreed-upon database, as it was called. Foremost among them perhaps was Senator Charles Mathias (R-Maryland), who made it his main issue in talking with the Soviets. He noted that in his home state of Maryland when someone bought strawberries at a market they wanted to verify that the berries on the bottom of the basket were as fresh as those on the top. At last the Soviets relented, again in the latter stages of the negotiations. Thus was repealed, by NTM, in the words of the Soviet ambassador, "400 years of Russian history."[3]

Avoiding Definitions

Senator Glenn shared this deep senatorial interest in verification. In the summer of 1977 in Geneva he suggested that perhaps there ought to be a definition of NTM put into the treaty. At this point President Carter had not yet prevailed in the long bureaucratic struggle in the U.S. government to declassify the fact that the United States was using reconnaissance satellites for intelligence collection and arms control verification. The U.S. delegation strongly suggested that Senator Glenn not raise this issue with the Soviet ambassador. Nevertheless, Senator Glenn raised the subject in his private meeting with Soviet ambassador Semenov, by now Soviet chief SALT negotiator for nearly eight years. Semenov was shocked. The only response he could come up with was, "Minerva's owl [the fount of wisdom] flies only at night."[4] The Soviets wanted nothing to do with defining or describing NTM.

However, eventually the U.S. administration generally described NTM in the article-by-article analysis of the treaty that it sent to the Senate in preparation for ratification hearings. It stated that NTM constitutes a broad range of systems for collecting intelligence. Such systems include, inter alia, photoreconnaissance satellites, the ships and aircraft that are used to monitor Soviet missile tests, and ground stations, such as the large U.S. radar on Shemya Island in Alaska. From the careful wording it was clear that other unspecified systems also contribute to U.S. NTM capabilities.

Telemetry Encryption

As mentioned earlier, the monitoring of Soviet missile telemetry was another major verification issue associated with SALT II. U.S. ground-based intelligence collection systems—then based in northern Iran—had for several years been intercepting the telemetry signals broadcast by Soviet missiles back to Soviet missile engineers on the ground during test flights. The data transmitted by these signals reported on all aspects of the operation of the missile during flight and how all the components were functioning so that the engineers could effectively analyze the operation of the missile in flight. By intercepting and studying these signals, U.S. intelligence analysts were able to gain a highly accurate understanding of the capabilities and performance of Soviet strategic missile systems. After a time, perhaps with the assistance of the Boyce/Lee espionage ring regarding U.S. high-altitude SIGINT satellites, the Soviets realized that the Americans were doing this and began to encrypt the signals. The U.S. Intelligence Community made it clear that one of its highest priorities in the SALT II negotiations was to get this situation turned around. This proved to be a very contentious issue, which was eventually taken out of the hands of the SALT delegations and discussed in the secretary of state–foreign minister channel.[5]

After a lengthy negotiation on this subject, agreement was reached at the last ministerial meeting of the SALT II process in December 1978. It consisted of an agreed-upon interpretation of the clause containing the prohibition on deliberate concealment from NTM of verification, carried over from SALT I. It barred any telemetry encryption that impeded verification. Also included was any other form of denial of telemetric signals, such as by recording the signals onboard the missile and recovering the capsule containing the information ejected by the missile during flight. Thus, while SALT I established the principle that satellite monitoring was legal under international law and appropriate for arms control treaty verification and that such monitoring would be protected from interference and deliberate concealment designed to diminish its effectiveness, SALT II established the concept that NTM needed and would have cooperative measures in order for it to truly do its job: for example, the missile and launcher type rules and the provision on telemetry encryption.

Throughout the strategic arms negotiation process, verification was, in spite of the contributions of NTM, always a big-ticket item. For example, in 1973 when Fred Ikle became director of the Arms Control and Disarmament Agency (ACDA), he reorganized the bureaus of the agency and established a verification bureau to be a sort of watchdog on SALT. He placed recognized conservatives, who were at best skeptical of the SALT negotiations, in the leadership positions of the bureau. Generally, it was viewed at the time as essentially a political act, but by casting aspersions on U.S. NTM (i.e., intelligence) capabilities, these individuals registered their opposition to the SALT process. It was a not uncommon tactic to oppose arms control by questioning, without necessarily having any basis, the verifiability of an agreement.

When Paul Warnke became the ACDA director under President Carter, in the spring of 1977, he did his own reorganization and in the process, abolished the verification bureau. Several months later in Geneva, in a meeting with the Soviet deputy SALT negotiator, the

U.S. deputy negotiator raised generally the subject of verification. The Soviet official replied, "But I thought that you Americans had abolished verification."[6] The verification bureau was reestablished by the Reagan administration, and it remained an inviolable part of the ACDA until the agency's absorption by the State Department in 1999. Thereafter, as a result of congressional pressure, it became a separate bureau in the State Department, where it remains in spite of a subsequent reorganization.

SALT II Ratification Issues

In spite of the continued advances made during the 1970s in U.S. NTM capabilities, such as the launching of the KH-11 real-time imaging reconnaissance satellite system, as well as the inclusion of type rules and a database in the treaty text, SALT II treaty verification was controversial during the ratification debate. Senator Howard Baker, the Senate minority leader, announced his candidacy for president during the ratification process and based his short-lived campaign on opposition to the SALT II treaty. The Senate Foreign Relations Committee held extensive hearings on the treaty, with verification a major subject. The committee held perhaps the longest treaty markup session in history, extending over several days, with Senator Glenn pressing hard on verification. The committee eventually voted in favor of the treaty by nine to six, Senator Glenn, and of course Senator Baker, voting against it.

Some senior nongovernmental observers, many of them former officials, had in 1976 formed an organization called the Committee on the Present Danger that, among other things, was highly critical of the SALT process. The committee argued that in spite of the efficacy of NTM, the type rules, and the telemetry provision, SALT II still was not "adequately verifiable." And in the months immediately prior to the ratification process, which began in late June and extended over the second half of 1979, the Shah of Iran was deposed by the Iranian Revolution led by Ayatollah Khomeini. As a result, the

United States lost its two principal ground-based telemetry monitoring installations in northern Iran (this was subsequently remedied by a new installation in western China, but not soon enough to help SALT II).[7] Several of the leaders of the Committee on the Present Danger eventually took prominent arms control jobs in the Reagan administration.

A number of factors contributed to the failure of the United States to ratify SALT II. While questions about verification had an important role, along with Soviet troops in Cuba, the Iranian hostage crisis, and the Soviet invasion of Afghanistan, the real reason for the failure was the fact that the SALT II treaty became caught up in the presidential politics of 1980. Republicans accused the Carter administration of underestimating Soviet capabilities and intentions as well as allowing the United States to fall behind in the arms race. Nevertheless, SALT II was informally observed by the Carter and Reagan administrations, as well as by the Soviets, until some six months beyond the date when it would have expired by its own terms in 1985. The U.S. Intelligence Community continued to be asked to monitor Soviet strategic nuclear forces and developments under the terms of the treaty, despite the absence of a ratified document.

Following this episode, the Reagan and George H. W. Bush administrations were determined to enhance U.S. NTM capabilities with improved systems, as well as to go beyond NTM to verify agreements. In the INF and START negotiations that began in the early 1980s and concluded in 1987 and 1991, respectively, the United States began to press for on-site inspections to supplement NTM monitoring.

Supplementing NTM Capabilities

Over the years, the increasingly detailed provisions of strategic nuclear arms control treaties required additional cooperative measures and obligations to supplement verification by NTM. However, the Soviets typically dragged their feet and resisted becoming more transparent.

INF Treaty

During the early years (1981–83) of the Euro-missile negotiations, known as the INF negotiations, and the START negotiations, little progress was made on verification or anything else. The Soviets appeared to be playing a political game in the hope of convincing NATO countries in Europe through public diplomacy and overt threats to halt NATO's plan to deploy new missiles to counter the Soviet SS-20 intermediate-range missiles facing Western Europe. When the first deployment of NATO's new Pershing (P-II) ballistic missiles occurred in Germany in the fall of 1983, the Soviets walked out of the INF negotiations. This move seemed to be their ultimate effort to pressure the NATO countries to halt their deployments.

Prior to the Soviet walkout, the United States had pressed hard for Soviet acceptance of the principle of on-site inspections, of course supported by NTM. This was partly an outgrowth of the SALT II ratification debate in Washington and partly because the limitations being pursued were even more ambitious than those in SALT II and likely could only be "effectively verified" (the Reagan administration replaced "adequately" with "effectively" as being somehow better or at least different) with the help of on-site inspections.

When the Soviets apparently concluded that their walkout had done more harm than good to their cause and agreed to return to the negotiating table in early 1985, the verification issue remained in the forefront. The United States eventually urged the abolition of all INF systems with ranges of 1,000 kilometers to 5,500 kilometers, which constituted the borderline of strategic systems, both in Europe and Asia, and then added the shorter-range missiles, above 500 kilometers in range, to the list of missile systems to be destroyed. The U.S. position called for baseline inspections of deployments and close monitoring of production and elimination, thereby making on-site inspections essential. The Soviets resisted for a time, but in October 1986 at the summit meeting in Reykjavik, Iceland—a watershed of arms control—General Secretary Gorbachev, for the first time for the Soviet Union, agreed to the principle of on-site inspections to verify the emerging INF Treaty. Nothing was ever the same thereafter. This fundamental change in position opened the door to the INF, START, and Conventional Armed Forces in Europe treaties, as well as to the Chemical Weapons Convention of 1993—all of which incorporated extensive on-site inspection measures.

The situation changed dramatically in Geneva as a result. Double global zero was agreed to, that is, all INF systems would be banned worldwide for the United States and the Soviet Union. Far beyond the agreed-upon database of SALT II, large amounts of information on INF systems were exchanged by the two sides. A Soviet colonel said after a major data exchange toward the end of the INF negotiations in the fall of 1987: "If I had handed over to the American side last week the information that I presented today I would have been shot."[8] As a result of the understanding reached that the INF Treaty would provide for the total elimination of these systems, the United States modified its requirements for a verification regime by dropping the provision for stationing inspectors outside all INF missile production and assembly plants, limiting it to one plant, and limiting short-notice, on-site inspections to declared INF facilities.[9]

On-Site Inspections

On-site inspection procedures were established in the context of the INF Treaty as a supplement to NTM. The objective was to verify the data in the initial information exchange through inspections of INF missile bases to verify the initial numbers, to inspect the elimination process as a means of verifying that all declared missiles were destroyed, and to conduct final base close-out inspections to verify the closure of bases after their missiles have been eliminated.

The on-site inspections were meant to have a synergistic relationship with NTM capabilities. Both sides recognized that even inspectors on the ground can be spoofed by a clever cheater, so provisions were included that would use on-site inspection to fill in gaps in NTM and vice versa.

The principal Soviet INF ballistic missile, the SS-20, was similar to the Soviet intercontinental-range strategic missile, the SS-25, except it lacked the SS-25's third stage. Both were land-mobile and built at the same production plant, so the United States insisted that the treaty provide for on-site inspections using X-ray equipment at this production plant to ensure that SS-20s were not being illegally constructed along with SS-25s. For the sake of reciprocity, Soviet inspectors were to be given the same inspection rights at a U.S. missile production facility, even though this problem did not exist on the U.S. side. Once again it took some time to convince the Soviets that such inspections were both necessary and feasible, especially given Soviet access to U.S. information as well as their penchant for secrecy and resistance to transparency. At one point in Geneva, the U.S. delegation invited the Soviet delegation to a demonstration of how such a monitoring system would work using a production facility mock-up, including a model train. After politely listening, the senior Soviet military officer said only one thing—that it would take a major change before anything like that would become possible. It is interesting to note that within two years, the two sides were installing on-site monitoring equipment that was able to x-ray real train cars. Much of the credit probably should go to Gorbachev, who after meeting with President Reagan in Reykjavik in the fall of 1996, agreed that on-site inspections should be incorporated into the verification activities for future arms control agreements.

To further support the solution of the SS-20/SS-25 problem, the two sides agreed to add a provision to the verification article (article XII, paragraph 3) of the treaty to enhance observation by NTM of verification. This clause provided that upon six hours' notice, up to six times a year during the three-year INF missile-elimination period of the treaty, the United States could request the sliding roofs of all garages for SS-25 ICBMs to be opened and all missiles displayed on their launchers in the clear—where they could be viewed by NTM and verified to be SS-25s and not SS-20s. Such measures applied only to SS-25 bases that were not former SS-20 bases, given that the latter would already be inspected under the treaty.

But in this first comprehensive on-site inspection regime in the nuclear arms control field, ultimate reliance remained with NTM for verification. Despite the potentially useful information derived from on-site inspections, it is possible for the party being inspected to conceal its activities. Thus, when negotiating arms control treaties, the United States usually considers all possible and feasible cheating scenarios to ensure that the verification provisions being negotiated, in conjunction with NTM, make it as difficult as possible to cheat. If the bar can be raised high enough, the other party or parties to the agreement may conclude that the cost and risk of cheating are too high. Even if successful cheating is possible, the gain will not be worth the effort nor militarily significant. For example, article IV of the INF Treaty prohibited the production and flight testing of missiles systems to be eliminated under the treaty. Thus, even if the on-site inspection verification regime missed a number of covert missiles, their value would dramatically decline over time due to the lack of flight testing of the missile. This flight-testing provision was judged to be verifiable through the use of NTM (e.g., by the collection of telemetry).

Confidence-Building Measures

Despite the addition of extensive data exchanges, various confidence-building measures such as the aforementioned requirement that the roofs of mobile missile launcher garages at missile bases be opened upon request, and the provisions of various extensive on-site inspections, the INF Treaty faced a skeptical audience during its ratification hearings. One issue was the Intelligence Community's uncertainty regarding the total number of SS-20 intermediate-range ballistic missiles that had been produced and, therefore, the number available to the Soviets as reserve missiles. Using the Defense Intelligence

Agency's estimate, which was at the high end of the range of uncertainty, Senator Jesse Helms accused the CIA and the Department of State Bureau of Intelligence and Research of having underestimated the number of missiles in the force. Those that exceeded the number in the operationally deployed force presumably would be secretly available to the Soviets even after they had destroyed all operational missiles. This, he claimed, proved that the treaty could not be verified. The second issue involved the fact that the treaty did not require accountability for the destruction of the warheads from the destroyed SS-20 missiles, which in theory meant that the Soviets could add those warheads to their longer-range ICBMs, thereby increasing the threat to the continental United States.

In defense of the treaty, Secretary of Defense Frank Carlucci explained that uncertainties were common in intelligence estimates of military forces and that any hidden SS-20s would soon be useless to the Soviets without periodic flight testing, which was banned by the treaty. Both he and Ambassador Paul Nitze testified, along with Intelligence Community officials, that our NTM would be able without a doubt to detect any flight testing of SS-20 missiles. Intelligence officials were careful to explain that the Intelligence Community could monitor many aspects of the treaty well, with some important limitations. However, they emphasized that it was not the responsibility of the Intelligence Community to declare whether the treaty was verifiable; that was a policy determination. These testimonies went a long way toward satisfying the Senate on the SS-20 issue. However, it took a report by the Senate Select Committee on Intelligence to make the determination that the Intelligence Community could monitor the INF Treaty and to argue that the treaty was verifiable.[10]

START I

The step from the INF Treaty to START was a logical but large one. The INF Treaty is verified by a combination of on-site inspection and NTM. START established cooperative verification. The basic provisions for NTM were almost unchanged from SALT I, but START I is replete with type rules, counting rules (as explained earlier), intrusive inspections, and cooperation in verification and large exchanges of data. It provides that each party will make missile telemetry freely available to the other in appropriate circumstances.

In its detailed complexity, START I is a lawyer's dream. There is a dizzying array of documents. There is, of course, the treaty proper, complicated in and of itself, which directly states the primacy of NTM. There are in addition thirty-eight statements of agreement on such subjects as the nontransfer of strategic offensive arms, SS-11 reentry vehicle attribution, strategic offensive arms operation outside national territory, the relationship between START I and the INF Treaty, throw-weight limitations (referring to the weight of the payload of a strategic missile) of new types of strategic missiles before the eighth flight test, and reimbursement of the cost of the telemetry tape exchange. In START I, there is a simple flat ban on the encryption of telemetry—so it can be easily read by NTM whether a missile is sea-based or land-based—and provision for the exchange of telemetry tapes in some cases, a far cry from the secrecy permeating the SALT I agreements and the unratified SALT II treaty. START I contains an annex of definitions of 124 terms for the purposes of the treaty.

In addition, there is a highly complex protocol on procedures governing the conversion or elimination of strategic offensive arms and providing for on-site monitoring of these processes. There is an even more complex protocol on on-site inspections and continuous monitoring activities—the verification protocol (with twelve annexes on various technical issues and activities). There is a protocol on notification to assist verification. There is a protocol on ICBM and submarine-launched ballistic missile throw weight and intrusive procedures to determine and attribute throw-weight values to specific types of missiles and to verify these values. There is an entire protocol on telemetric information that provides the procedures for access to missile telemetry for verification purposes. And there is, among many other additional documents, a very lengthy memorandum of understanding setting forth the voluminous basic information on strategic offensive arms exchanged by the two parties and on which the treaty is based.

START I came into force in December 1994, and in December 2001, at the end of the seven-year period of reductions, the United States and Russia announced that the treaty had been fully implemented. Russia had become the functioning treaty partner with the United States as a result of the collapse of the Soviet Union on Christmas Day 1991. The Lisbon Protocol to the treaty, which was signed in May 1992, substituted Russia, Ukraine, Belarus, and Kazakhstan for the Soviet Union—the four states with Soviet strategic offensive arms left on their territories—as START I treaty partners with the United States. The Lisbon Protocol specified that Ukraine, Belarus, and Kazakhstan agree not to have strategic offensive arms located on their territories and to join the NPT as non-nuclear-weapon states. This left Russia as the effective strategic partner with the United States.

START II

START II, which never came into force, was signed by Presidents Bush and Yeltsin in January 1993. The idea was that it was to be a short agreement based on the procedural and verification provisions of START I, which principally would reduce U.S. and Russian levels of strategic offensive arms well below those of START I. Thus, it contains no general verification provisions but is based on those of START I. START II does, however, contain unique on-site inspection arrangements for such things as warhead inspections of missile systems, particularly for those missiles whose warhead payloads have been "downloaded" (e.g., the number of warheads actually deployed on specific missiles, such as the U.S. D-5 submarine-launched missile and the Russian SS-19 ICBM, could be less than the number they are capable of carrying).[11] In addition, special measures were included to monitor the modification of the MIRVed SS-18 silos so that they could contain only smaller, single-warhead missiles, in compliance with the START II ban on MIRVed ICBMs.

There are also elaborate bomber rules that would permit some nuclear-capable bombers of a type to be "reoriented" to a conventional role as long as they had "observable" (by NTM) differences. In SALT II the concept of "functionally related observable differences" was created to distinguish between strategic bombers with and those without long-range cruise missiles, which were included under different limits. The START II concept was that these differences only need be observable by NTM; that is, the difference didn't have to be functionally related, or in other words, essential to their distinguishable new role. But bomber verification was a Soviet/Russian problem, not an American one, because the Soviet/Russian bomber fleet was always a minor element of their strategic forces aimed at the United States.

The primacy of NTM for the United States, even in the cooperative verification regimes envisioned by the START I and START II treaties, was emphasized by the Deputy Director for Intelligence (DDI) of the CIA in his February 28, 1995, testimony before the Senate Foreign Relations Committee on START II. He said: "We are cautious about becoming totally dependent upon Russian information or cooperation to perform our monitoring tasks." He added: "We believe that it will be vitally important, to the extent possible, to utilize our array of technical collection systems as a means to ensure an independent capability to monitor the treaties."[12]

The DDI further emphasized in his testimony that the Intelligence Community had assisted in the design of treaty provisions to enhance the effectiveness of NTM: "We helped design specific [START II] Treaty provisions that were included in the Treaty to complement our monitoring capabilities and thereby inhibit cheating. Information resulting from these provisions interacts synergistically with data from our national intelligence means to enhance monitoring capabilities. For instance, the procedures for converting SS-18 silos for use by smaller, single warhead missiles makes undetected reconversion to SS-18 launchers virtually impossible. The process would thus be consuming, difficult, expensive, and easily observed."[13]

Last, it should be noted that even though START I has been fully implemented, its verification provisions live on, at least until 2009. The Strategic Offensive Reductions Treaty of 2002, which calls for the United States and Russia to reduce the number of their strategic offensive arms on operational alert by December 31, 2012, itself contains no verification provisions. However, its second article asserts that START I remains in force according to its terms (until 2009—fifteen years from 1994—after which it may be extended by successive five-year periods by mutual consent of the parties). This provision ensures a relationship between the United States and Russia whereby the START verification regime—fundamentally based on NTM supplemented by a vast on-site inspection regime and cooperative measures—is available to provide the foundation for confidence, transparency, and predictability in further strategic offensive arms reductions.

NTM Centrality to U.S. Treaty Monitoring

Despite the addition of on-site inspections, data exchanges, and cooperative measures in various agreements, NTM remains the ultimate guarantor of a treaty's verifiability for the United States. Because negotiated treaty provisions necessarily educate potential cheaters on the best way to circumvent any agreement, the United States relies heavily on its own largely undefined NTM capabilities to protect U.S. national security.

In addition to the technical systems normally associated with NTM, the U.S. Intelligence Community continually collects and analyzes information on the activities of its potential foes. Indeed, one of the basic justifications for the Intelligence Community is its role in preventing surprise attacks. Thus, assisting policy makers in devising the most effective provisions to inhibit cheating on agreements is in effect an intelligence function. From the initiation of policy consideration of a possible negotiation through an agreement's ratification and implementation, the U.S. Intelligence Community uses all of its resources to protect U.S. national security interests. Monitoring arms control agreements is one of its most important responsibilities, but its responsibility goes beyond the task of monitoring traditional strategic nuclear forces. As discussed in chapter 8, its responsibilities increasingly include the challenge of monitoring foreign programs and activities associated with the proliferation of nuclear and other weapons of mass destruction.

7

"National Technical Means" Goes Multilateral

AFTER THE LEGALIZATION of monitoring using national intelligence

capabilities through the bilateral U.S.-Soviet SALT agreements,

verification by NTM became the principal enabler and precondition

of almost all subsequent arms control treaties, including some mul-

tilateral accords. If a particular limitation on armaments of the United

States and the Soviet Union was considered a desirable constraint,

one that would add to U.S. security, it was considered acceptable to pursue only if it was verifiable by NTM. Of necessity that meant that the agreements of the 1970s had to focus on limiting relatively large observable items, such as missile launchers. With the advent of treaty provisions such as the limitation on telemetry encryption in the late 1970s and the addition in the late 1980s of on-site inspections and cooperative measures, it became possible to negotiate more qualitative limits on strategic nuclear forces, such as the number of missile warheads, missile throw weight, and other system characteristics that went beyond monitoring the levels of large force components. Roughly at this same time NTM also became a significant factor in conventional forces and nuclear-testing multilateral arms control negotiations (see Appendix B for details).

Seabed Treaty

As mentioned earlier, the Seabed Arms Control Treaty of 1971 was perhaps the first multilateral arms control treaty to explicitly refer to verification by national means. However, a distinction needs to be drawn between "national means of verification" and "national technical means of verification" established under the SALT I agreements. The former is an old term used as early as the nuclear test ban negotiations of 1958–62. At that time it primarily referred to the use of monitoring systems located in third countries, such as seismic detection systems located in say, Norway, that could monitor underground nuclear explosions in the Soviet Union. There were also signal detection systems located in third countries that monitored communications— at least to some degree—in the Soviet Union as well as the People's Republic of China. These unspecified systems were recognized as legitimate verification systems, inter alia in a speech by the Soviet ambassador to the Eighteen Nation Disarmament Committee (a predecessor of the present-day Conference on Disarmament) in 1962.[1] The United States, the United Kingdom, and the Soviet Union had just completed over three years of negotiations on a nuclear test ban without result because of the impasse over verification. The Eighteen Nation Disar-

mament Committee was created in March 1962, but the impasse continued, thereby leading to President Kennedy's proposal in June 1963
for the limited test ban treaty, which, as discussed in chapter 2,
bypassed the problem of the verification of underground tests.

"National technical means of verification," in contrast, was
invented during the SALT process in the early 1970s and was initially designed to refer to monitoring by space-based reconnaissance
systems. Once accepted, these space-based systems, along with other
intelligence capabilities, opened the door to much more comprehensive arms control agreements since they allowed the negotiating parties to see into one another's territory and detect critical
military activity. The reference in the Seabed Treaty was not intended
to be specific, however; rather it simply meant that a party could initially verify the treaty by whatever legal national means available to it.

Nuclear Non-Proliferation Treaty

Probably the first real multilateral use of U.S. NTM was the gradual
practice by which the International Atomic Energy Agency (IAEA)
began to utilize information obtained by the United States in its efforts
to monitor peaceful nuclear activities under the NPT. For example, U.S.
reconnaissance satellites detected, in 1992, two suspicious waste-
storage sites near the 5-megawatt nuclear reactor at Yongbyon, North
Korea. This reactor had been briefly shut down in 1988, long enough
to extract spent fuel rods sufficient to reprocess enough plutonium
for one to two nuclear weapons. Upon receipt of the satellite photographs of these two sites, the IAEA staff asked North Korea for permission to inspect them. Upon refusal by North Korea, the IAEA staff
referred the matter to the agency's board of governors, and the pictures (slightly reduced in resolution) were made available to the board.[2]
Because of the continuing refusal of North Korea to allow IAEA staff
to inspect pursuant to the NPT Safeguards Agreement between North
Korea and the IAEA, the IAEA board referred the case to the UN Secu-

rity Council for consideration of sanctions. Before the Security Council could act, North Korea announced its withdrawal from the NPT, thereby beginning the long series of nuclear crises with North Korea that continue to this day.

CFE Treaty

In 1989–90, NATO and Warsaw Pact countries negotiated and concluded the Conventional Armed Forces in Europe (CFE) Treaty. This treaty was aimed at ending the long Cold War conventional arms confrontation in Europe and finally bringing real peace to the continent. The CFE Treaty is arguably the agreement that ended the Cold War and established the basis for peace in Europe for decades to come. It provides limitations for all countries with forces on the European continent (defined as the area between the North Atlantic and the Ural Mountains), and it is based on a vast on-site inspection regime.

But NTM is not overlooked, indeed it is recognized as one of the mainstays of the CFE Treaty. And since this is a treaty that limits military equipment on the territory of every one of the thirty treaty parties, the relevant treaty provisions declare that in addition to the on-site inspection provisions, the treaty is to be verified by "national and multinational technical means of verification." The provisions established in SALT I requiring noninterference with NTM and prohibiting deliberate concealment measures, which could diminish the efficacy of NTM, were applied to multinational means as well. Thus, the treaty contemplates verification not only by U.S. and Russian NTM but also by satellite or other verification systems owned by several countries or by the European Union. Today there exist commercial services, available to anyone, that can provide pictures from space of almost anywhere on earth. Thus, while verification of the CFE Treaty is based largely on its on-site inspection regime, the ultimate guarantor is spaced-based reconnaissance owned by one or perhaps several of the parties.

CWC

The next major multilateral arms control agreement, the Chemical Weapons Convention (CWC) of 1993, based its verification arrangements entirely on its comprehensive on-site inspection provisions. It contains no reference to NTM. And indeed, vessels containing the prohibited chemical agents—poison gases—could be quite small and perhaps effectively verified only by inspections. However, the United States would never have entered this agreement—given the fact that chemical weapons have actually been used in war (World War I, Ethiopia in 1935, Yemen in 1967, and the Iran-Iraq war of the 1980s)—without believing with confidence that its NTM could detect significant military troop training to prepare for the battlefield use of these weapons and would therefore provide timely warning of a potential adversary's capabilities and intentions. Some argue that the absence of references to NTM does not exclude it from being used, but other countries would most certainly object to its overt use in the CWC context because of the lack in the treaty of specific authorization for the use of NTM data.

BWC

As indicated earlier, the international community did not attempt to negotiate verification provisions for the Biological Weapons Convention (BWC) until the 1990s. Even then efforts to create a verification regime for the BWC were very difficult. The nature, developmental process, and manufacture of biological agents cannot be reliably monitored with NTM alone; monitoring requires on-site inspections. Beginning in 1995, negotiations commenced in Geneva, Switzerland, to develop a verification protocol for the BWC. Six years of negotiations of a BWC verification and inspection protocol led to the tabling of a draft text by an interested group of states on July 23, 1999. It called for routine plant inspections on two weeks' notice. The draft protocol was nearly complete when in December 2001, at the BWC

Review Conference, the United States blocked the completion of the negotiations on the protocol and unilaterally terminated the negotiations over the violent objections of U.S. Allies. This was done to a considerable extent because of objections from the U.S. biotech industry, which was concerned that inspectors might somehow gain access to trade secrets during inspections. This episode demonstrates the need to find new techniques for bringing remote, technical monitoring capabilities to bear on chemical and biological weapon proliferation issues.

International Reservations Regarding NTM

Despite the vital contribution that NTM has made in bilateral U.S.-Soviet/Russian negotiations on strategic nuclear weapons systems during and immediately following the end of the Cold War, as well as to the CFE Treaty, the international community has been less comfortable with the idea of using national intelligence capabilities to monitor international arms control agreements as well as to fight proliferation. Some see it as a compromise of sovereignty and of giving too much influence to the United States, with its vast intelligence-monitoring capabilities. The issue came to a head in the early-mid 1990s as the international community sought to negotiate several arms control agreements. As noted above, NTM was not even discussed during the negotiation of the CWC and is not mentioned in the text of the convention. However, the role of NTM was openly debated during the negotiation of the CTBT, and the use of NTM data is included in the text of that treaty. Moreover, the IAEA director, General Mohamed ElBaradei, has admitted that his agency welcomes and uses national intelligence data from its member states to facilitate its international monitoring of nuclear programs.[3]

CTBT

The CTBT of 1996—which has not yet come into force—has a verification arrangement that is unique. The international community's primary reliance is on the International Monitoring System (IMS), a worldwide remote monitoring complex operated by the Comprehensive Nuclear-Test-Ban Treaty Organization in Vienna (see Appendix E for details on the IMS). But for suspicious cases provision is made for the use of on-site inspections. A request for such an inspection by a state party to the treaty is to be referred to the Executive Council (comprised of fifty-one treaty parties) created by the treaty. To authorize an inspection, a requesting party must gain the support of thirty of the fifty-one members. But in making its case, the requesting party is explicitly authorized by the treaty to use information obtained by NTM and/or the IMS. This was a major issue pushed by the United States. The United States explained that NTM in the CTBT context goes beyond reconnaissance satellites to include systems similar to those being installed as part of the IMS.

Efforts to achieve agreement on the use of NTM monitoring of the CTBT proved difficult. Recognizing that remote technical monitoring would be ideal for monitoring nuclear test activities at known and suspected test ranges, several delegations (principally France, Russia, the United States, and the United Kingdom) argued that it was essential to include any available NTM data to ensure that the CTBT verification regime would be comprehensive and credible. Opponents argued that the international monitoring system planned for the CTBT would be sufficient and that permitting the inclusion of national data would make the playing field unbalanced in favor of those countries with sophisticated NTM capabilities. Moreover, some (principally China and Pakistan) argued that national intelligence monitoring had been used in the past to unfairly accuse some countries of misdeeds. Therefore, opponents sought to prevent the use of NTM data; their fallback position was a call to define those NTM capabilities that would be permitted for nuclear test monitoring and to regulate their use to ensure sufficient accountability and to prevent any abuse in the use of such data.

All of this led to what was the first-ever open debate regarding the role and nature of NTM. NTM advocates argued that opponents to the inclusion of NTM in the treaty needed to take a long view of the NTM issue. Admitting that at one time NTM capabilities had been the sole province of the two superpowers, they argued that commercial satellite imagery, for example, was now becoming available to all countries that wished to purchase it. Thus, over time in the context of a treaty designed to be in force indefinitely, the playing field would eventually even out. They also argued that any definitions of NTM would necessarily limit the effectiveness of the treaty's verification regime, given that new technologies and monitoring techniques would undoubtedly be developed over the decades. Moreover, data from NTM would help raise the barrier to cheating, because most potential cheaters would not know, in contrast to the IMS, how good NTM capabilities of individual countries really are and, therefore, what cheating scenarios might actually succeed.[4]

In the end, those favoring the inclusion of NTM data won out, but their opponents ensured that the bar to abusive use of NTM, especially as the basis for requesting on-site inspections, was high enough to protect their security concerns. Although the CTBT has set a precedent for the inclusion of NTM in an international arms control agreement, the treaty has yet to enter into force. It is not clear, therefore, how influential this precedent will be in any future international negotiation.

When the U.S. Senate finally agreed to hold hearings on the CTBT in the fall of 1999, Senate Democrats unknowingly stepped into a political trap set by the Senate Republicans for the Clinton administration. Setting aside the political issues at play, some of the opponents of President Clinton and the treaty claimed, based on Intelligence Community testimony, that the treaty was unverifiable because current technology was not able to detect nuclear tests down to zero yield, as required by the treaty. Seeing that the administration was unable to make the case for the treaty, the opponents seized upon the verification issue as a convenient club to kill the treaty's prospects. This was done despite the fact that the Clinton administration, recognizing the limits of NTM and the CTBT's IMS to provide 100 per cent monitoring confidence, had included certain conditions that would provide the United States the ability to resume testing should our national security require it. Although political considerations dominated the debate, some in the Senate considered U.S. national capabilities to monitor nuclear tests as insufficient to guarantee U.S. national security under a permanent ban.

FMCT

As part of the grand bargain struck during the negotiation of the NPT in the late 1960s, the declared nuclear weapons states agreed to reduce and eventually eliminate their nuclear stockpiles in return for all other countries' agreeing to forego nuclear weapons. During the NPT Review and Extension Conference in 1995, the nuclear weapons states further agreed, along with a CTBT, to negotiate a Fissile Material Cutoff Treaty (FMCT)—a ban on the production of fissile material that could be used for weapons. It became clear that the non-nuclear-weapon states viewed these negotiations as disarmament initiatives aimed at restraining existing nuclear arsenals, while the nuclear weapons states saw them also as nonproliferation initiatives. Despite continued calls from the UN General Assembly to launch such negotiations, serious negotiation of an FMCT has never gotten under way, due mainly to objections from various countries in the Conference on Disarmament—initially India and then China. More recently, the United States has voiced reservations about the verifiability of an FMCT, given the inherent challenge of verifying the production and stockpiling of nuclear material. Most conclude that on-site inspections would be required to verify such a production ban, but studies are also under way to determine what contribution NTM might bring to this challenge. In some ways, the verification challenges posed by a potential FMCT mirror those faced during the CWC and BWC negotiations; that is, the activity of interest is likely to be conducted inside buildings that have other legitimate purposes.

Thus, NTM has been included in multilateral agreements along with on-site inspections only on a selected basis. Its potential effectiveness depends on the activities and items to be limited or banned. Unfortunately, the post–Cold War world is marked by increased proliferation concerns and activities that appear to be straining the limits of traditional NTM capabilities. Moreover, the international community continues to be wary, principally because of concerns that a few advanced countries have an unfair advantage in such capabilities and, if unchecked, might unjustly harass other countries. Over time, however, NTM capabilities are becoming more available to an increasing number of countries. The challenge is in developing techniques and procedures that will be more effective in monitoring the more difficult targets posed by proliferation activities, along with negotiating treaties that include provisions to complement the technical capabilities of existing NTM to provide credible and effective verification.

8

Monitoring the Proliferation of Weapons of Mass Destruction

AS IMPRESSIVE AS their contribution has been, it is not enough to focus only on what intelligence capabilities have contributed to monitoring foreign military forces and arms control agreements in the past. Twenty-first century international security challenges associated with the proliferation of nuclear, chemical, and biological weapons, along with their delivery systems, demand the full and immediate attention of the U.S. Intelligence Community.

The requirement to monitor existing nuclear weapon stockpiles around the globe remains, but we are faced with growing efforts by some states to develop clandestine WMD programs and to proliferate the technologies associated with such weapons, if not the weapons themselves.

We must learn how to use national and multinational capabilities effectively to counter attempts by terrorists to acquire and use WMD. The monitoring tasks are somewhat different and in some ways more difficult than those faced during the Cold War, and new intelligence sources and methods may be required. Imagery and communications intelligence would appear to be of particular use in tracking, locating, and preventing efforts by state and nonstate actors to develop and/or acquire WMD, and particularly nuclear weapons and related technology.

Therefore, the Intelligence Community's challenges in the twenty-first century will include requirements to monitor existing stockpiles of WMD (especially nuclear weapons), small clandestine WMD programs, WMD proliferation efforts, and potential terrorist acquisition and use of one or more types of WMD. Except for possibly the last, these are not entirely new tasks. Proliferation has been a national security issue for the United States for decades. However, following the end of the Cold War and the collapse of the Soviet Union, efforts to pursue clandestine WMD programs and to increase WMD technologies seem to have been given a boost. Therefore, we believe it is important, following the discussion of the previous chapters, to at least mention how these developments pose new challenges to the Intelligence Community, challenges that in some cases are similar to but generally go beyond the use of NTM to monitor arms control agreements.

WMD

The term "weapons of mass destruction" is often misunderstood and incorrectly used as a synonym only for nuclear weapons. Generally speaking, however, the term refers to nuclear, chemical, and biological weapons. In the military arena, it may also cover the delivery means (i.e., missiles, aircraft, etc.). In the context of terrorism, of course, the delivery means may be an individual person.

Nuclear devices (i.e., bombs and missile warheads) truly are weapons of mass destruction, given their destructive power through blast, heat, and irradiation. Chemical weapons, however, are normally viewed by military planners as tactical battlefield weapons. They can affect only a relatively small area, although, like nuclear weapons, their effects are immediate. Biological weapons are unique in that they may have only delayed impact, which allows the agents to be spread far.

Both chemical and biological weapons are often referred to as the poor man's nuclear weapons since the infrastructure to produce them is cheaper and more easily obtained than that for nuclear weapons. Chemical and biological agents should more appropriately be called weapons of mass terror and casualties rather than destruction, although both U.S. and Soviet militaries studied ways to militarize such agents. In the hands of terrorists, of course, any of the three WMD types would create panic and havoc.

The activities and processes associated with the clandestine development and deployment of WMD programs by proliferating states are quite different in magnitude from those associated with the traditional, large military forces of the declared nuclear weapon states (i.e., China, France, Russia, the United Kingdom, and the United States). Chemical and biological weapons, for example, can be produced in fertilizer and pharmaceutical plants respectively without any unique signatures. Almost with the flip of a switch, legitimate civilian and defensive chemical and biological production facilities and processes can produce offensive WMD agents; the facilities involved are not necessarily unique.

Monitoring Existing Nuclear Stockpiles

It seems evident that those countries that now possess nuclear weapons systems will retain them for the foreseeable future. Despite significant strides that the United States and the Soviet Union/Russia have made in reducing the size of their operational strategic forces and eliminating nuclear weapons systems over the past two decades, neither views it possible yet to give up its nuclear forces in total. Similarly, the other internationally recognized nuclear weapon states (China, France, and the United Kingdom), along with the newly self-declared nuclear weapon states (India and Pakistan and perhaps North Korea) can be expected to hold on to (and in several cases actually increase) their arsenals in the coming decade (and the same can be said for the undeclared arsenal of Israel). Thus, remote technical monitoring, through both existing arms control agreements and nonproliferation arrangements as well as unilateral efforts, will continue to be a valuable tool for both the international community and individual nation-states in monitoring the disposition and evolution of existing nuclear weapon arsenals.

Russia's Nuclear Stockpile

Despite the collapse of the Soviet Union and the end of the Cold War rivalry between the United States and the Soviet Union, the requirement to monitor the former Soviet nuclear arsenal remains a high priority for U.S. national security. However, the control and safety of former Soviet weapons became more critical as the result of the threat posed by the proliferation of nuclear and other WMD among so-called rogue states and to international terrorist groups.

After the dissolution of the Soviet Union in late 1991, not only did the large former Soviet arsenal of nuclear weapons systems continue to exist, but initially after the breakup the weapons were located in four newly independent sovereign countries. U.S. focus shifted from the possibility that these systems might be used against the United States in an armed conflict to concerns about positive command and control as well as the physical security of the former Soviet nuclear weapons and weapons-grade nuclear material. Fortunately, as described in chapter 6, the various strategic nuclear arms control treaties signed by the former Soviet Union remain in force, and their verification provisions require continued monitoring—through both NTM and on-site inspections.

At the end of the Cold War, the Soviet Union had some twelve thousand strategic nuclear warheads and bombs in its arsenal in addition to many thousands of other nuclear weapons.[1] Because the Soviets had deployed their strategic nuclear forces widely across the Soviet Union to optimize targeting and survivability, the strategic weapon systems were now located in the newly independent countries of Belarus, Ukraine, Kazakhstan, as well as the Russian Federation. Because of historic nationalist and ethnic tensions, there arose potential threats to the control and safety of these weapons systems. Russia desired to retain positive control of all of the nuclear weapon systems, especially the warheads. Through initiatives such as the Nunn-Lugar threat-reduction legislation, the United States offered assistance to Russia to accomplish this objective.[2] This legislation provided funding to certain programs in Russia to enhance the security of nuclear weapons and fissile material and to undertake elimination of such weapons and material. There was considerable fear that now-unemployed Soviet nuclear experts would sell their services and former Soviet "loose nukes" would end up in the hands of renegade nationalist leaders, ethnic terrorists, or rogue states.

Fortunately, the Russian Federation agreed to abide by the strategic nuclear treaties signed by the USSR that called for significant reductions and elimination of weapons systems. As mentioned, some of the obligations of those treaties were expanded through the Lisbon Protocol to include Belarus, Ukraine, and Kazakhstan so that verification activities could legally continue within the borders of the newly independent states where former Soviet nuclear forces remained. Thus, monitoring of the disposition and eventual consolidation of the nuclear weapons systems in Russia became a priority both for weapons security and to ensure that provisions of the various arms control treaties were being adhered to by the relevant parties. In addition, the tactical nuclear weapons, which were scattered all over the fifteen republics of the Soviet Union, were recalled to the Russian Republic at the time of the collapse of the Soviet Union.

China, India, and Pakistan

In addition to ongoing efforts to monitor through arms control agreements and other arrangements Russia's stockpiles of nuclear weapons and materials, there is concern related to China's continuing efforts to increase the size of its relatively small nuclear arsenal. We must continue to monitor the Chinese arsenal to avoid any strategic surprises and to ensure that no Chinese nuclear material gets into the wrong hands. Similarly, the international community must keep focus on the even smaller Indian and Pakistani nuclear arsenals, given the tensions that exist in South Asia between these two neighbors and the ongoing efforts of international terrorists to get their hands on weapons-grade nuclear material, if not nuclear devices themselves.

MONITORING SMALL-SCALE CLANDESTINE WMD PROGRAMS

The challenge of monitoring small, clandestine nuclear, chemical, or biological weapons programs is different in scope and scale from the challenge the Intelligence Community faced in monitoring large Soviet nuclear forces during the Cold War. Intelligence capabilities were optimized against the development, testing, production, and deployment stages of relatively large military programs—the kind that can make a strategic difference in the balance of power and on the battlefield.

In contrast to monitoring strategic weapons production, testing, and deployment, traditional technical intelligence collection capabilities are of less value against the research phase of such programs. Most covert nuclear weapons programs have been detected at the time when reactors were being built and certainly when actual nuclear testing took place. Prior to these points, clandestine human agents were likely to be the best source for the existence and status of nuclear weapon research programs. Even in the case of Iraq, the Intelligence Community understood correctly in 2002 that Iraq had not tested a nuclear device and did not posses any nuclear weapons. Moreover, it had monitored the test flights of missiles that exceeded UN-mandated range limits. However, clearly it was much more difficult to determine the status of Iraq's chemical and biological weapons programs.

Due largely to their unique character, chemical and biological weapons programs, particularly those that are covert and in the early stages of development, are much harder to detect than nuclear programs. Legitimate fertilizer and pharmaceutical plants can produce, respectively, offensive chemical and biological agents. Only through on-site inspections or human agents can one hope to detect the existence of such weapons programs. If such weapons were to be used on a military scale, we would likely detect training and preparations. However, the challenge of detection is magnified when the intelligence target is a small amount of chemical or biological agent delivered by an individual terrorist.

Monitoring Nuclear Proliferation

Concerns about the proliferation of nuclear weapon programs go back to at least the early 1960s, but the passing of the Cold War world has led to renewed efforts at nuclear proliferation. The post-1991 Gulf War discovery by UN inspectors of advancements made in Iraq's clandestine nuclear weapons program added urgency to international efforts to counter such proliferation.[3] It was clear that U.S. and other nations' intelligence had missed key indicators of the Iraqi nuclear program. This led to U.S. efforts to enhance its capabilities to more diligently monitor weapon developments in countries of concern other than the former Soviet republics.

In contrast to chemical and biological weapons programs, clandestine nuclear programs are somewhat harder to mask, given the size and unique nature of the infrastructure required to enrich or reprocess fissile material for use in weapons. Moreover, some type of aircraft or missile delivery system is normally associated with nuclear warheads or bombs. Thus, activities associated with these systems can normally be monitored remotely, at least to some degree. Nevertheless, much of the research activity for nuclear weapons can take place out of sight and without unique signatures.

Moreover, the world has now realized after discovering the extent of the black market nuclear proliferation network run by Pakistani scientist Abdul Qadeer Khan, the reputed father of the Pakistani nuclear weapon, that otherwise innocent-looking commercial transactions can, in fact, mask proliferation activities.[4] The uncovering of Dr. Khan's activities led to the discovery of nuclear technology shipments from North Korea to Libya. This in turn led to the exposure of the Libyan nuclear program and its renunciation by Libya. As a result of these events, intelligence collection and analytic capabilities must be used in an aggressive manner to guide interdiction activities, such as have taken place under the U.S.-led Proliferation Security Initiative. Such activities will be done in conjunction with UN Security Council Resolution 1540, which calls on all states to take measures to prevent the proliferation of nuclear weapons and material.

India Goes Nuclear

India, which for decades had refused to join the NPT and which had conducted what it claimed to be a peaceful nuclear explosion in 1974, appeared in the 1990s to be showing a renewed interest in nuclear weapon developments. Politically, India's leaders began to insist that India too needed to be recognized as a great power, which many interpreted to mean the possession of nuclear weapons.

In 1995, Washington raised with New Delhi its concern over what appeared to be preparations for an Indian nuclear test. The next year, India refused to join consensus on and sign the CTBT, which did not bode well for India remaining a non-nuclear-weapon state. Then in 1998, India exploded several nuclear devices and announced that the tests had been successful. Pakistan soon followed, which led to the addition of two new self-declared nuclear weapons states to the international scene. Although the United States had spotted what appeared to be Indian preparations for nuclear tests in 1995, it failed to detect preparations for the 1998 tests, although as stated earlier it did detect the actual tests.[5] It appears that India learned some important lessons regarding how to mask its test activities from the 1995 episode. Subsequently, the United States and India agreed to a strategic partnership arrangement that in part includes the resumption of nuclear technology trade in exchange for separation of military and commercial nuclear facilities in India. This arrangement raises challenging monitoring problems, and it remains to be seen what its effect will be on the international nuclear arms proliferation regime.

Iraqi Nuclear Weapon Program

Given Iraq's unaccounted-for WMD-related material and efforts to mislead and conceal its activities from the international community prior to 2003, the U.S. Intelligence Community, in conjunction with many other intelligence services and experts around the world, believed that Iraq had both chemical and biological weapons stockpiles. There was greater uncertainty regarding the status of Iraq's nuclear weapon program; no one believed that Saddam yet had the bomb after his program was dismantled by UN inspectors following the 1991 Gulf War, but experts differed on how much progress he had made toward reconstituting his nuclear weapon program after he stopped all UN inspections in 1998.[6] Nevertheless, because of ambiguity and uncertainty, no one could be sure what the facts were and what subsequent inspections would uncover. It now seems clear that Iraq had not made nearly as much progress as the United States and others believed.[7]

This episode demonstrates the difficulty and limits of national and multinational remote technical capabilities to collect against such clandestine programs, especially in the research stage. In contrast to the Cold War days when it was possible, albeit still difficult, to monitor large weapons systems with the help of arms control agreements, remote monitoring of clandestine WMD programs, especially chemical and biological programs that can be housed in relatively small facilities, must be joined by information collected through credible on-site inspections and reliable human sources with appropriate access to maximize the chances of early detection.

North Korea's Nuclear Weapon Program

International efforts to understand the full extent of North Korea's nuclear weapons program continue to be hampered by the insular and closed nature of the Kim Jong Il regime. North Korea provides as difficult a target to penetrate as one can imagine. In addition to being a society that is largely closed off from the rest of the world, North Korea's terrain and extensive tunneling make it extremely difficult to remotely monitor certain clandestine military activities. Except, for

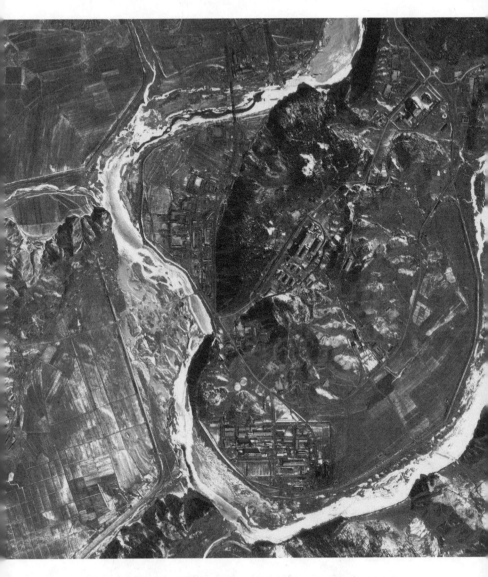

Yongbyon Nuclear Facility, North Korea. Reconnaissance satellites have been used to follow efforts by the North Koreans to extract and reprocess nuclear material as part of their program to develop and produce nuclear weapons. Credit: Getty Images 1684260

A close look at Yongbyon Nuclear Facility, North Korea. Credit: Getty Images
1834576

example, missile launch facilities, which due to their size are harder
to conceal, it is difficult to locate hidden facilities without some tip-
offs. Moreover, North Korean concealment and deception practices
make it difficult to uncover the full extent of the program.[8]

No one now doubts that North Korea has at least a few nuclear
weapons. Indeed, Pyongyang announced on October 9, 2006, that it
had carried out an underground nuclear test and subsequently stated
that it might conduct additional tests. A week later, on October 16, the
Office of the Director for National Intelligence issued a statement confirming that North Korea had conducted an underground nuclear explosion based on analysis of air samples containing radioactive debris that

Natanz Nuclear Facility, Iran. Reconnaissance satellites image the construction and operation of nuclear facilities around the world in an effort to detect and analyze efforts by countries such as Iran to proliferate the development and production of nuclear weapons. Credit: DigitalGlobe/Getty Images 71212650

were collected on October 11. Thus, North Korea gave the international community new evidence of its nuclear weapon capability and became the third, after India and Pakistan, new self-declared nuclear weapon power in the last decade. However, sophisticated remote intelligence sensors were required to confirm Pyongyang's claim.[9]

Iran's Nuclear Weapons Program

Although it appears that Iran has yet to produce nuclear weapons, the international community has become increasingly concerned that Iran may be attempting to develop the infrastructure that would permit them to do so in future years. Published intelligence estimates put this capability at six to ten years in the future; nevertheless it is a worrisome possibility. IAEA inspectors have found no proof of a dedicated weapons program, but it has uncovered evidence of Iran's efforts to circumvent its obligations under the NPT. Given Teheran's hostility toward the United States and its support for international terrorism, there is heightened suspicion that Iran, as was the case with Saddam's Iraq, will turn to WMD programs, especially nuclear, to ensure its national security.

Concealment, Denial, and Deception

The Indian and Iraqi episodes particularly demonstrate the challenge that any monitoring effort faces in terms of overcoming concealment and deception measures employed, especially when associated with clandestine weapons development activities. It appears that the Indians had taken careful steps leading up to the tests in 1998 to avoid repeating the procedures and physical signatures apparent in 1995. And Saddam's Iraq was legendary in its efforts to conceal and to deceive UN inspectors throughout the 1990s and just prior to the U.S. military invasion in March 2003. It is safe to say that other potential proliferators are taking or will take similar measures to mask their activities and intentions associated with clandestine WMD programs.

Although the Soviets had used extensive and varied concealment and deception measures to mask their military activities during the Cold War, the various strategic arms control treaties adopted by the United States and Soviet Union enhanced the effectiveness of their respective monitoring and verification activities. Indeed, as mentioned in chapter 6, some of the later treaties, in addition to on-site inspections, even required the parties to display their weapons systems at various times to ensure adequate verification (see Appendix B). It was clear that their agreement to such measures was motivated, at least in part, by the desire to enhance strategic stability by preventing misunderstandings and miscalculations.

Unfortunately, would-be proliferators in the post–Cold War era are unlikely to be as accommodating and cooperative as the Soviet Union finally became toward the end of the Cold War. The international community's experience thus far with countries such as Iran, Iraq, Libya, and North Korea casts doubt on their willingness to make it easy for others to know exactly what they have or are developing in terms of WMD capabilities. Although Libya is now willing to be more transparent, the same cannot yet be said for Iran and North Korea. Furthermore, Israel has demonstrated for decades the effectiveness of ambiguity in its strategic posture, neither confirming nor denying its nuclear weapons capabilities. And countries have learned that they can sometimes defeat monitoring efforts through cooperation with other countries. The possible nuclear explosion in the South Atlantic in 1979 may very well be a case in point. Despite the statements of some South African officials that it was a joint Israeli–South African test of a nuclear device, Israel has never officially addressed the issue.[10]

Even when a country comes under the close scrutiny of the international community, it is not always possible even with the best intelligence capabilities and on-site inspections to achieve an accurate understanding of what that country is doing or has accomplished in terms of its clandestine weapons programs. The status of the Iraqi WMD programs prior to U.S. military action in early 2003 is an excellent example. Despite years of on-site inspections by the United Nations and IAEA and close monitoring by individual countries, it appears that most experts failed to understand the actual progress (or lack thereof) made by Saddam's regime to reconstitute its WMD capabilities, particularly chemical and biological, after the 1991 Gulf War and subsequent UN inspections. Saddam's desire to develop

WMD was well understood and accepted, but it was more difficult figuring out exactly how much progress he had made in reconstituting his capabilities after terminating UN inspections in 1998.[11] Many argue that if the UN and IAEA inspection teams had been allowed to complete their assignments before the March 2003 invasion of Iraq, the chances of a more precise understanding of Iraq's WMD capabilities would likely have been greater.

Monitoring Terrorist Efforts to Acquire WMD

Perhaps the most difficult arena today for intelligence collection and analysis is monitoring international terrorist activities, particularly those aimed at acquiring WMD, where individuals rather than large organizations or weapon systems are the prime threats. For the most part they are indistinguishable from ordinary individuals and strive to blend in with the rest of society. However, this is not a task for traditional NTM, in the sense that there are no existing treaties with terrorist organizations that require verification. To be sure, monitoring the activities of rogue states and countering the proliferation of WMD capabilities to terrorists is a high-priority task, and dedicated intelligence resources are required for the effort. But this is a qualitatively different task from what we have thus far described in this book with regard to verification of treaties between or among states.

What most troubles many governments is the nexus between rogue-state proliferators and the terrorist organizations they support. Hardly anyone expects terrorists to develop or even possess nuclear weapons arsenals in the traditional sense. But, they undoubtedly seek sufficient nuclear material and explosives to create radiological weapons that, when detonated, would create panic and contaminate a significant area with radiological poison. And, it is entirely possible that a terrorist organization some day may come into possession of one or two nuclear weapons, through theft, the assistance of a rogue state, or by assembling a crude device itself using fissile material obtained on the black market.

Chemical and biological weapons appear to be more suitable for terrorist use, given the relative ease of production and concealment through dual-use plants and the relatively small size of lethal doses required to create panic. And such weapons pose a greater challenge in terms of detecting their deployment because their signatures are unlikely to provide a tip-off prior to an attack.

The foregoing discussion makes clear that, except in the case of monitoring traditional nuclear weapons arsenals, remote technical intelligence monitoring capabilities must be augmented by other collection means. In the international arena, this normally involves on-site inspections—conducted by the United Nations or other international organizations. In the national context, this may involve human-source collection activities, some of which are clandestine in nature, although open-source information can also contribute to a fuller understanding of proliferation efforts. The bottom line is that synergy among collection disciplines is a must in order to defeat efforts to conceal clandestine WMD activities from national or international monitoring efforts, and effective international cooperation and sharing of information are essential.

Both international and national intelligence and law-enforcement efforts require careful and thorough analysis to derive the greatest benefit from all information collected, whether from remote technical sensors or human sources (i.e., inspectors or agents). The collection of more data is not necessarily the answer in all cases, but rather more sophisticated processing, in-depth research, and analysis of the data already available.[12] Proliferated equipment must still be shipped from source to recipient, and international interception of such shipments is possible through established procedures, such as the U.S.-led Proliferation Security Initiative. Often only tenacious analysts thinking outside the box will make the associations among data that are required to see the true picture. However, success in connecting the dots correctly is never assured, so competitive analysis and second-guessing are required to challenge assumptions.

9

Conclusion

AFTER THE USE of the first atomic bombs in 1945 at the close of World War II and the subsequent nuclear standoff between the United States and the Soviet Union during the Cold War, all-out warfare as had been witnessed during the first half of the twentieth century became unthinkable to most people. Nevertheless, nuclear arsenals grew, and there were close brushes with nuclear war during the Cold War. Gradually the two superpowers came to understand that total war would mean the complete destruction of their societies and perhaps world civilization. This understanding was summarized in the Communique at the end of the 1985 Summit Meeting between President Ronald Reagan and General Secretary Mikhail Gorbachev in the Summit Communiqué, which stated in part that "a nuclear war cannot be won and must never be fought."[1]

Of course, in the history of warfare, nations have attempted to acquire the most destructive weapons that they could and as many of them as possible so as to maximize their strength. And this was true of nuclear weapons as well. The United States built nuclear weapons during World War II because of great concerns that Nazi Germany would acquire them. The Soviet Union sought nuclear weapons as an effect of Cold War competition, the United Kingdom and France to ensure great-power status for themselves, and China so as to be able to resist both the Soviet Union and the United States. But many other states developed nuclear weapon programs. Sweden had a vigorous program, Switzerland twice voted by national referendum to build nuclear weapons, Argentina and Brazil had serious programs, and South Africa built six weapons before the government of Prime Minister de Klerk terminated the program and destroyed the weapons that had been built. Nuclear weapons have added to national prestige, and giving them up or undertaking not to acquire them has not been a natural action for sovereign states.

However, the advent of nuclear weapons has made war so potentially destructive that advanced nations have had to devise some way to control this technology or risk self-destruction. A very dangerous and unstable situation developed by the late 1950s, and there was a real risk of a devastating nuclear war. As mentioned, limiting strategic arms was tried many times in the 1950s and early 1960s, but these efforts failed because of the inadequacy of reliable verification. This changed with the advent of the revolution in national intelligence capabilities described in this book. By the early 1970s, the verification of strategic arms limitation agreements became possible through the use of new, remote technical monitoring systems that permitted the superpowers to gradually gain enough confidence to bring the nuclear arms race under control.

Before this achievement, the proliferation of nuclear weapons had become a growing concern. President Eisenhower had recognized the risk and the stakes involved. In 1953, in his famous "Atoms for Peace" speech to the United Nations, Eisenhower noted that "the dread secret and the fearful engines of atomic might are not ours alone" and that "the knowledge now possessed by several nations will eventually be shared by others—possibly all others."[2] When President Kennedy took office in 1961, he asked the outgoing secretary of state, Christian Herter, which country would be next to acquire nuclear weapons. The answer was Israel and India. President Kennedy tried especially hard to prevent the Israeli bomb, reasoning that if the United States could not dissuade its ally Israel, how could it say no to Germany? German acquisition of nuclear weapons would have been a serious provocation to the Soviet Union, fraught with dangerous consequences. President Kennedy truly feared that nuclear weapons would sweep the world, and during his administration there were predictions of as many as twenty-five to thirty nuclear weapons states, with nuclear weapons integrated into their arsenals, by the end of the 1970s. If this had happened, there would be many more today. More recently, in September 2004, IAEA director Mohamed ElBaredei said that "40 countries or more now have the know-how to produce nuclear weapons."[3] In a world with nuclear weapons so widespread, every conflict would run the risk of going nuclear.

Fortunately, most of the countries that have the capability to produce or acquire nuclear weapons have not chosen to do so. In 1960, after the first French nuclear weapon test in the Sahara, banner headlines in French newspapers declared "Vive la France" and "Vive de Gaulle." Yet by the time of the first Indian test explosion in 1974, India received worldwide condemnation, and New Delhi hastened to explain that it had been a peaceful test. The signing in 1968 and the entry into force in 1970 of the NPT took place between the French and Indian tests. The NPT converted a state's acquisition of nuclear weapons from an act of national pride in 1960 to an act contrary to the practices of the civilized world in 1974. In fact, there has been very little nuclear weapons proliferation since the entry into force of the NPT in 1970, far from what President Kennedy had feared. Besides the five nuclear weapons states recognized by the NPT (the United States, the United Kingdom, France, Russia, and China), two—Israel and India—were far along in their programs in 1970. The only additional states to truly acquire nuclear weapons since that time have been Pakistan and now North Korea. Central to this situation is the international norm against nuclear weapons proliferation established by the NPT augmented by efforts to prevent further proliferation.

President Eisenhower had also focused on the central importance of bringing the nuclear arms race between the United States and the Soviet Union under control. Not to do this "would be to confirm that two atomic colossi are doomed malevolently to eye each other indefinitely across a trembling world."[4] Seeking to bring this dangerous arms competition to an end, the Nixon administration began the first phase of the SALT negotiations. As appalling as the nuclear arms race became, especially in the late 1970s and early 1980s, the situation would have been far worse if not for the strategic arms agreements made possible, in part, by the development of sophisticated remote intelligence monitoring systems referred to as NTM. This eventually led to the strategic offensive arms reductions of the 1990s (incorporated in the START treaties) that are so important to the termination of the nuclear arms race and for the reinforcement of the NPT.

Thus, the practice of worst-case analysis during the nuclear standoff—which existed throughout the Cold War and led to close calls with nuclear war and the dangerous unchecked arms race that persisted for so many years—was gradually brought to an end. What permitted this to happen was in large part the revolution in national intelligence capabilities that provided a mutually acceptable means for the two adversaries to far more accurately understand the strength of the other side's forces and to develop and rely on arms control arrangements designed to limit, regulate, and eventually terminate the arms race.

The message of this book is that, by virtue of the development of reconnaissance satellite systems, along with other sophisticated intelligence collection technologies and analytic methodologies, to help the United States understand and avoid miscalculating Soviet strategic military capabilities and intentions, the United States (and later the Soviet Union) changed the course of history.

Data collected by these systems and then analyzed made it possible for the U.S. Intelligence Community to replace worst-case military assessments with better-informed analysis. For the first time states could peer into each other's interior and observe what was happening. Large items such as missiles, bombers, ships, units of troops, and tanks could be seen, located, and counted. Surprise warfare— such as the Nazi blitzkrieg—became more difficult and therefore less likely. One side could at last accurately measure the other side's strategic forces, at least in gross terms. In time this technology improved and became capable of observing smaller and smaller objects with improved resolution, which eventually made meaningful arms control treaties possible.

This revolution in technology and national monitoring capabilities helped bring the arms race to an end through the strategic nuclear arms control agreements, and to inhibit nuclear proliferation through various multilateral arrangements. As one author has concluded, "Intelligence played a crucial part in stabilizing the Cold War."[5] The world is less dangerous than it otherwise would have been at the commencement of the twenty-first century because of the invention of reconnaissance satellites and other types of intelligence capabilities. If a truly peaceful and stable world order is ever achieved, the advent of this technology beginning in the late 1950s will be regarded by future generations as a major historical turning point. These are capabilities that not only the United States but the international community as well must support, protect, and continue to develop to ensure appropriate monitoring and effective verification as long as WMD, particularly nuclear weapons, threaten lives, nations, and international stability. Confirmation of its nuclear weapon capability by North Korea's test in October 2006 and Iran's ongoing effort to achieve nuclear weapon status are only the latest examples of the continuing need for effective intellingence capabilities to monitor clandestine nuclear weapon programs.

Postscript

GIVEN THE SIGNIFICANCE of what has been achieved in technical

monitoring capabilities over the past sixty years, as described in this

book, it should be clear that the need to protect both the development

and operation of space-based and other reconnaissance capabilities

is critical to U.S. national security in the twenty-first century. National

monitoring capabilities, especially reconnaissance satellites, are

increasingly threatened by the possibility of an arms race in space, by which offensive ASAT capabilities could expand. It is of the greatest importance that this not happen and that space remain a sanctuary for these important national monitoring capabilities.

December 1, 2004, marked the forty-fifth anniversary of the signing of the Antarctic Treaty, which preserved the continent as a nonmilitarized, nuclear-weapon-free area—the first arms control agreement of the modern era. The debate that preceded the negotiation of that treaty is remarkably similar to contemporary discussions on the future of outer space. In the first half of 1950s, there were about a dozen countries vying for scientific, economic, and military interests in Antarctica, an uninhabited, borderless, and lawless land. In time, and after much debate, those twelve states—with others joining afterward—decided that the greater interests of all of the affected parties would be served best if the continent could be preserved for peaceful uses and that those interests could best be protected through a legal arrangement rather than the use or deployment of military forces.

Today, the international community is faced with similar questions about how to protect the assets associated with the use of outer space. Here again, we have a borderless realm rich in commercial, scientific, and military potential and questions about how best to preserve these assets. Will military deployments and the weaponization of space be required to defend critical space technology? Indeed, is—as some have suggested—the weaponization of space an inevitable evolution of current and historic realities?

A great deal rides on the answer to these questions. Scientifically, the stakes are quite high, with everything from the International Space Station to the Hubble telescope and the exploration of Mars potentially affected by instability and unpredictability in outer space. The commercial implications are even greater. But perhaps most important of all are the reconnaissance satellites that are the subject of this book, as well as those satellites designed to give early warning of missile attacks.

Similarly, it is also evident that outer space is becoming a more dangerous place. Several countries, including Russia and China along with the United States, have developed sophisticated ASAT weapons, and several others are thought to be seeking such weapon systems. If they continue to proliferate, ASAT weapons have the potential to dramatically undermine fundamental U.S. interests as well as world security.

The realization of the increasing vulnerability of the United States to attacks against space assets has caused some to encourage Washington to begin to deploy defensive weapon systems to protect those assets from new weapons. While this could appear to make sense on a basic level, a thoughtful analysis of the history of military development reveals flaws in this notion. Most important, modern history categorically demonstrates that effective defensive weapons systems will inevitably be countered by effective offensive systems, sparking an ever-spiraling arms race that ultimately leaves all sides less secure.

The Outer Space Treaty joined the Antarctic Treaty in a unique class of arms control agreements sometimes referred as nonarmament treaties. These agreements were intended to—and they have been successful—prevent the deployment of weapons in areas where they have not previously been present. Today, after more than three decades, space remains free of WMD.

It has been suggested that a legal regime to prevent the weaponization of space could be crafted simply by building upon the Outer Space Treaty. There may be some merit to this idea, especially considering the fact that the treaty has more than ninety states parties. However, the subject is complicated and there are many important interests to protect— telecommunications, navigation, and weather systems— but of the highest importance are those space assets used to verify treaty compliance and for intelligence. Ensuring noninterference with these assets is crucial to ensuring peace and security in the twenty-first century because of the central role they play in preserving confidence in the nonproliferation regime and in international security arrangements generally. President Reagan's devotion to the Russian adage of "trust but verify" was correct. Without space-based and other types of NTM, this would be impossible—a reality that U.S. and Russian negotiators were keenly aware of during the arms control and international security negotiations of the last thirty years.

Such considerations apply not only in the bilateral U.S.-Russian context but also to the broad range of international security concerns. It is important in this respect again to recall that the suspicions that Israel and South Africa might have conducted an atmospheric nuclear test in the South Atlantic during the late 1970s were driven by readouts from an American Vela reconnaissance satellite.

At present, space-based reconnaissance is regularly used to track activities that could be associated with programs to develop WMD in countries of concern around the world. This and other examples of monitoring are crucial efforts that we must never allow to be disrupted, especially not with relatively simplistic weapons systems that could someday be deployed. Given the relentless progression of technological development, ensuring that these monitoring and verification measures are protected is a reality that probably ultimately can only be achieved through international law.

The groundwork for such a comprehensive treaty-based regime has been laid, and the importance of this objective is clear. Much work remains, but the creation of a space regime, under which the international community decisively enshrines space as a peaceful environment and in the process ensures the long-term security of space-based intelligence collection, is the only thoroughgoing alternative to a weaponized space free-for-all in which the United States and the rest of the world would be rendered forever vulnerable to the vagaries and fluctuations of technology development and political instability, and in which international peace and security in the twenty-first century would be fundamentally undermined.

Appendixes

A. Glossary of Acronyms and Terms

The following acronyms and terms are commonly used when discussing arms control and NTM issues:

ABM Treaty. Anti-Ballistic Missile Treaty, signed as part of the SALT I agreements in 1972; the United States withdrew from the treaty in 2002

AFTAC. Air Force Technical Applications Center, which conducts U.S. monitoring of foreign nuclear programs and testing through operation of the USAEDS

BWC. Biological and Toxin Weapons Convention negotiated in 1972

CBM. Confidence-building measures included in some arms control agreements to augment NTM

CD. Conference on Disarmament, which is the international community's sole body for negotiating multilateral arms control agreements

Corona. Code word for the first successful U.S. photoreconnaissance satellite program

CTBT. Comprehensive Nuclear Test Ban Treaty, which was negotiated in 1996 but has yet to enter into force

CWC. Chemical Weapons Convention, which was negotiated in 1993 and entered into force in 1997

FMCT. Fissile Material Cutoff Treaty, an agreement that has never been negotiated but which would be intended to ban the production of weapons-grade fissile material

IAEA. International Atomic Energy Agency, which has responsibility for monitoring peaceful nuclear activities under the Nuclear Non-Proliferation Treaty

ICBM. Intercontinental-range ballistic missile

ICRC. International Committee of the Red Cross

IMINT. Imagery intelligence, which is derived primarily from air- and space-based reconnaissance systems

IMS. International Monitoring System, which was established to monitor nuclear testing activities under the CTBT

INF Treaty. Intermediate-Range Nuclear Forces Treaty, which was signed in 1987 and entered into force in 1988, bans all intermediate-range ballistic missiles and shorter-range (ranges of 500 kilometers and above) ballistic missiles

Interim Agreement. Signed and entered into force in 1972 as part of SALT I as an interim step toward a more permanent limitation on strategic offensive arms of the United States and USSR

IRBM. Intermediate-range ballistic missile, defined as those missiles with ranges between 1,000 and 5,500 kilometers

Keyhole. Code word used by the United States for satellite reconnaissance

LTBT. Limited Test Ban Treaty, signed and entered into force in 1963

MIRVs. Multiple independently targetable reentry vehicles

Monitoring. The process of tracking treaty-relevant activities of parties to an arms control agreement to verify compliance with the treaty; tracking the development of weapons programs

NIE. National Intelligence Estimate

NPT. Nuclear Non-Proliferation Treaty, signed in 1968 and entered into force in 1970

NTM. National technical means of verification

OSI. On-site inspection

PNET. Peaceful Nuclear Explosions Treaty, a companion treaty to the TTBT, which was signed in 1976 and entered into force in 1990

PSI. Proliferation Security Initiative

SALT I. Strategic Arms Limitation Talks, which led to the ABM Treaty and Interim Agreement on strategic offensive arms, both of which were signed and entered into force in 1972

SALT II. Strategic Arms Limitation Talks, which led to the signing in 1979 of a longer-term agreement limiting strategic offensive arms; the treaty never entered into force but was informally observed

SDI. Strategic Defense Initiative

SIGINT. Signals intelligence

SORT. Strategic Offensive Reductions Treaty, signed in 2002

Sputnik. The first class of Soviet artificial earth satellites first orbited in 1957

SR-71. The U.S. Air Force version of a fast, high-flying reconnaissance aircraft originally developed by the CIA as the A-12

SS-20. The Soviet intermediate-range nuclear ballistic missile, which had been deployed in the western and eastern USSR but which was eliminated under the INF Treaty

START I. Strategic Arms Reduction Treaty, which was signed in 1991 and entered into force in 1994, reduced U.S. and Soviet strategic offensive arms by about 50 percent

START II. Strategic Arms Reduction Treaty, the intended follow-on treaty to START I, signed in 1993 but which never entered into force because of the U.S. withdrawal from the ABM Treaty

State party. A country that has both signed and ratified a treaty

Telemetry. In this book, refers to radio signals reporting on performance transmitted from ballistic missiles and aircraft to engineers on the ground

TTBT. Threshold [Nuclear] Test Ban Treaty, which was signed in 1974 and entered into force in 1990

U-2. First high-flying reconnaissance aircraft operated by the CIA to overfly the USSR.

UNGA. United Nations General Assembly

UNSC. United Nations Security Council

UNSYG. United Nations Secretary-General

USAEDS. United States Atomic Energy Detection System

Verification. The efforts made by parties to a treaty to ensure mutual compliance

B. Texts of NTM Provisions in Arms Control Agreements[1]

The following provides the texts of the NTM provisions included in various bilateral and multilateral arms control agreements. There is no mention of NTM in the LTBT, BWC, CWC, or NPT. However, as stated in chapter 7, the IAEA does make use of NTM data from its member states to support its monitoring responsibilities under the NPT. Moreover, NTM data can be used to inform individual parties of a treaty about activities that are relevant to the treaty's provisions even if that data cannot specifically be used in compliance deliberations.

The inclusion of references to NTM in those treaties where it is specifically mentioned evolved over time. Such treaties normally include three basic provisions: (1) one that grants the right to states parties to the agreement to use national monitoring capabilities consistent with international law; (2) a second that requires countries being monitored to refrain from interfering with such monitoring; and (3) a third that prohibits deliberate concealment measures impeding verification by such monitoring capabilities. Additional details regarding these provisions are provided in some agreements.

Seabed Treaty

In 1971, the Seabed Treaty became the first multilateral agreement to include specific references to national monitoring. In Article III, paragraph 5, it states that "verification . . . may be undertaken by any State Party using its own means." And in paragraph 6, it states that "verification activities . . . shall be conducted with due regard for rights recognized under international law."

SALT I

In 1972, the U.S.-Soviet SALT I agreements (ABM Treaty and Interim Strategic Offensive Arms Agreement) were signed and include the first specific references to NTM. In their respective verification articles, they state (in paragraph 1): "Each Party shall use national technical means of verification at its disposal in a manner consistent with the generally recognized principles of international law." In paragraph 2, the agreements state: "Each party undertakes not to interfere with the national technical means of verification of the other Party operating in accordance with paragraph 1 of this Article." And in paragraph 3, they state: "Each Party undertakes not to use deliberate concealment measures which impede verification by national technical means of compliance with the provisions of this Treaty." These two agreements set the standard for most subsequent U.S.-Soviet arms control accords.

TTBT

In 1974, the United States and the Soviet Union signed a treaty limiting the underground testing of nuclear weapons. They adopted the SALT I language for the first two NTM paragraphs. The third paragraph requires the two parties to "consult with each other, make inquiries and furnish information in response to such inquiries."

PNET

In 1974, the United States and the Soviet Union also signed a treaty regulating the conduct of underground nuclear explosions for peaceful purposes. Similar to the TTBT text, in paragraph 1(a) of its verification article, the PNET states that each party shall "use national technical means of verification at its disposal in a manner consistent with generally recognized principles of international law." And in paragraph 2, it states: "Each Party undertakes not to interfere with the national technical means of verification of the other Party operating in accordance with paragraph 1(a) of this article."

SALT II

In 1979, SALT II was signed between the United States and the USSR, which included what had become the standard NTM language in the verification provision of bilateral strategic nuclear arms control treaties. However, the negotiators recognized that the increased complexity of this agreement required them to expand the noninterference and deliberate concealment provisions. They included specific bans on the use of shelters that would impede the ability of the other side to associate specific missile types with their launchers. SALT II also banned the deliberate denial of telemetric information through such means as the use of telemetry encryption designed to mask such signals when such denial would impede verification. Each of these prohibitions demonstrated how the two sides were using their NTM capabilities to monitor the other and a recognition that the denial of such information would impede verification and, therefore, confidence in the agreement.

INF Treaty

In 1987, the INF Treaty was signed and included the traditional NTM language from the earlier SALT agreements along with an obligation calling for cooperative measures, such as displaying upon request selected road-mobile missiles in their garages, to enhance observation by NTM. This provision was specifically focused on the challenge of monitoring Soviet road-mobile intermediate-range ballistic missiles, as long as they remained in the force, as well as long-range ground-launched cruise missiles. The INF Treaty also, for the first time, added on-site inspections to the formal verification regime.

CFE Treaty

In 1990, another modification to the standard NTM formulation was included in the CFE Treaty, a multilateral treaty between NATO and Warsaw Pact countries. It added "multinational technical means" to "national technical means" at the insistence of NATO Allies, who wished to make clear that states parties could jointly operate technical means of verification. Accordingly, the bans on interference and deliberate concealment applied to both national and multinational NTM.

START

In 1991, START was concluded. It expanded even further the specific details included in the SALT II treaty regarding bans on the denial of telemetric information from test flights of missiles. In addition to direct prohibition of telemetry encryption, it includes explicit bans on jamming, using narrow directional beaming, and encapsulation through ejectable capsules or recoverable reentry vehicles. START also included confidence-building measures to enhance verification by NTM and on-site inspections modeled after the INF Treaty.

CTBT

In 1996, the CTBT was signed and included the right to use NTM. However, it slightly modified the standard phrasing of the basic right by stating that "no State Party shall be precluded from using information obtained by national technical means of verification in a manner consistent with generally recognized principles of international law, including that of respect for the sovereignty of States." These two modifications reflected the sensitivity among those countries that believed they were at a disadvantage in the NTM capabilities available to them and sought every means to prevent abuse by States with more capable NTM. The CTBT also included a noninterference provision, but it did not include a ban on deliberate concealment. Opponents of NTM argued that the noninterference provision covered everything.

Finally, in the discussion of requests for an on-site inspection, the treaty stated that a request shall be based on "information collected by the International Monitoring System, on any relevant technical information obtained by national technical means of verification . . . , or a combination thereof." Allowing NTM data to be used solely as the basis for an on-site inspection was a major achievement by the pro-NTM advocates during the negotiation. However, the fact that the CTBT has yet to enter into force begs the question of how important the CTBT precedent will be in terms of including NTM language in any subsequent multilateral treaties.

SORT

SORT, also referred to as the Moscow Treaty of 2002, is silent on verification. However, in the preamble it notes that the two sides are "mindful of their obligations under the START Treaty," and article II states that "the Parties agree that the START Treaty remains in force in accordance with its terms." Therefore, it is reasonable to conclude that all of the detailed verification provisions and obligations contained in START, including on-site inspections and others, apply to the reductions called for under SORT, at least until those provisions expire in 2009 if not extended.

C. Chronology of Key U.S. Reconnaissance Capabilities

Reconnaissance Aircraft

RB-29	1945–47	Used to monitor early Soviet nuclear testing
RB-47	1948–56	Used to monitor along the periphery of the USSR
U-2	1956–Present	Used to overfly the USSR and subsequently to monitor Soviet military activity during the Cuban missile crisis. Still in use for a variety of missions
SR-71	1964–2000	Used to monitor the periphery of the USSR and other areas of intelligence and military interest
WRC-35	1960–Present	Used to monitor nuclear testing and for open skies under the Conference on Security and Cooperation in Europe.

NOTE: A variety of other aircraft were designed or modified for reconnaissance missions during the Cold War

Photoreconnaissance Satellites

Corona	1959–72	Includes KH-1 to KH-4 systems described below
KH-1	1959–60	Had a nominal ground resolution of 40 feet (i.e., the ground-size equivalent of the smallest item visible on the imagery)
KH-2	1960–61	Had a nominal ground resolution of 10 feet
KH-3	1961–62	Same ground resolution as the KH-2
KH-4	1962–63	Equipped with two cameras to provide stereoscopic imagery. Became the primary workhorse of the Corona program and evolved into three models. By 1967 the KH-4B had a nominal ground resolution down to 5 feet
KH4A	1964–69	
KH4B	1967–72	
KH-5	Early 1960s	Provided mapping services for the U.S. Army

KH-6	1963	Abandoned due to disappointing performance
KH-8	1966	Designed for high-resolution detailed photography, with estimated ground resolution of 1 inch
KH-9	1971	Designed for broad-area search, with estimated ground resolution of less than 6 inches
KH-11	1976	First electro-optical imaging system capable of directly transmitting images to ground station, with estimated resolution of less than 1 inch
KH-12	1986	Improved KH-11 system[2]

Corona Satellite Program

The Corona program consisted of a series of satellites with increasingly more accurate cameras that provided coverage of the Soviet Union, China, and other areas from the Middle East to Southeast Asia. From its start in the late 1950s until its termination and replacement by more advanced systems in 1972, the Corona program provided U.S. policy makers with timely and accurate information on the USSR and China. Within a few months of the Soviet downing of the CIA's U-2 aircraft in May 1960, the United States launched its first successful reconnaissance satellite. During that first mission, the satellite provided more photographic coverage of the Soviet Union than all previous U-2 missions during the preceding four years.

Since the early 1960s a significant percentage of finished intelligence—those analyses passed to policy makers—has been derived largely from data provided by reconnaissance satellites. They were used to assess military strength and grain harvests, but their greatest utility was in monitoring the development and deployment of Soviet strategic nuclear forces for U.S. defense needs and to verify Soviet compliance with arms control agreements. Corona's initial major accomplishment was the imaging of all Soviet medium-range, intermediate-range, and intercontinental ballistic missile launching complexes, as well as the missile test range north of Moscow; coverage of the main Soviet construction site for ballistic missile submarines at Severodvinsk, which allowed the United States to follow the construction and deployment of the Soviet Navy; and it uncovered construction of the Soviet antiballistic missile defense system around Moscow.

Although it was generally understood, the U.S. government did not acknowledge that it used satellite systems and imagery for intelligence and arms control verification purposes until 1978 when it was officially made public by President Jimmy Carter after a long intragovernmental review that led to the decision. In 1995 President Clinton ordered the declassification of historical intelligence imagery from the early satellite systems, and the declassified photographs were sent to the National Archives, with copies going to the U.S. Geological Survey for scientific and environmental uses.[3]

Follow-On Satellites and Other U.S. Collection Systems

Once the United States, and presumably the Soviet Union, had mastered the basics of satellite photoreconnaissance, they began to make significant improvements in their systems, especially in the ground resolution of their cameras and the duration of their flights. In 1966 the United States began orbiting the KH-8, high-resolution satellites for detailed analysis of targets. This was followed in 1971 by the KH-9 "Big Bird" satellite, which was able to provide broad-area searches with somewhat less resolution. These two systems became the workhorses of U.S. overhead imagery until the advent of the long-sought electro-optical system, which was able to transmit images directly to a ground station rather than periodically ejecting film capsules that then had to be developed before analysts could examine them.

According to one author, who comprehensively investigated U.S. NTM system capabilities in the mid-1980s—at the height of strategic competition with the USSR—those systems included (1) Big Bird KH-9 and KH-11 photographic and multispectral scanning satellites, which produce and instantaneously relay a continuous flow of detailed images of every square inch of Soviet territory by day or night, and active imaging radar satellites, which produce the same images, at almost the same level of detail, when clouds obscure the view of the others; (2) a network of over-the-horizon radars that have been tracking and measuring Soviet missiles in test flights at ranges of thousands of miles since at least 1955; (3) more than four thousand electronic ground intercept stations; (4) a large fleet of intelligence ships and a force of more than four hundred specialized reconnaissance aircraft to perform photomapping and collect radar, signals, and telemetry intelligence from every border of the Soviet Union; and (5) electromagnetic satellites, from orbiting Ferrets to geostationary Rhyolites, which record and instantaneously relay every electronic signal broadcast anywhere in the Soviet Union.[4]

D. U.S. Atomic Energy Detection System (USAEDS)

Beginning in the late 1940s, the United States began to monitor the nuclear tests of other countries. This effort, which includes various types of technical sensors located in the air, on the ground, and underwater, evolved into the U.S. Atomic Energy Detection System. The system is operated by the U.S. Air Force Technical Applications Center (AFTAC), which is located at Patrick Air Force Base in Florida. The center operates twenty-four hours a day, 365 days a year.[5]

As agreements to limit nuclear testing have been negotiated over the years, AFTAC has been charged with monitoring the LTBT, the TTBT, and the PNET. In addition, AFTAC provides assistance to the IAEA and serves as the U.S. laboratory responsible for supporting the agency's analysis of samples.

In the case of the CTBT, AFTAC began sending experts to advise the U.S. delegation during the negotiations in Geneva and provided leadership in developing the CTBT's International Monitoring System. AFTAC experts remain deeply involved in supporting the efforts of the CTBT's Provisional Technical Secretariat (PTS), both by operating and maintaining those USAEDS stations that are also part of the IMS, and as a resource of expertise for the PTS to ensure a smooth buildup of the IMS.

E. CTBT International Monitoring System

Negotiation of the CTBT led to the establishment of the IMS, which is a remote technical monitoring system that mirrors to a large degree the types of national sensor capabilities that the United States and selected other countries had independently developed to monitor nuclear test activities. In contrast to national systems, which typically focus on particular regions of concern, the IMS was designed to provide uniform global coverage so that no country would conclude that it was singled out for international monitoring.

Although the IMS is quite advanced in its development, it will have only limited ability to monitor nuclear testing activities in the foreseeable future because of the entry-into-force and political hurdles the CTBT faces. Key countries, including China, India, Iran, Pakistan, North Korea, and the United States, have refused to sign and/or ratify the treaty for various national security reasons. Until they do, there is no international legal obligation for countries to refrain from nuclear testing activities, unless such activities also contravene their obligations under other treaties, such as the NPT. Thus, national monitoring of nuclear test activities by individual countries, including any cooperative ventures groups of countries may establish, is the principal means at the present time to monitor nuclear testing. In part it was the concern that the CTBT may never enter into force that caused some U.S. senators to vote against the treaty in 1999 and to call for the enhancement of U.S. national monitoring capabilities.

The CTBT's IMS consists of 321 stations located around the world in some 250 locations (some sensors are collocated to reduce operating costs) in about ninety countries so as to provide roughly equal global coverage. Sensors from the four technologies are to be deployed as follows:

- seismic: 50 primary sensors (i.e., continuously operating) and 120 auxiliary sensors (i.e., intermittent/ on-demand operations) to detect shock waves through the earth;
- hydroacoustic: 6 hydrophone sensors located underwater and 5 T-phase (essentially seismic) sensors located on islands to detect shock waves through the oceans;
- infrasound: 60 sensors to detect shock waves through the atmosphere;
- radionuclide: 80 particulate sensors, 40 of which are initially to be collocated with sensors for collecting noble gas as well as particulate samples carried by prevailing winds. The radionuclide stations are to be supported by certified laboratories capable of analyzing samples upon request.[6]

CTBT negotiators estimated that the detection capability of the IMS, once fully built and operating, would be about 1 kiloton of yield, nonevasively tested. Thus, there was a recognized gap in detection capability between the zero ban and the international technical monitoring system to be built.

F. U.S. Intelligence Community

The U.S. Intelligence Community is a collection of sixteen agencies and organizations within the executive branch that conduct diverse intelligence activities in support of U.S. policy-maker requirements. These agencies and organizations are responsible for the development and operation of collection systems and activities as well as for the analysis of all-source data to understand the threats to U.S. national security.

Most of the IC organizations belong to the various policy departments of the executive branch and support their specific missions. The Department of Defense contains the majority of these components in support of military planning and operations. Only the CIA was created to be independent of any policy department in order to serve the intelligence needs of the President and National Security Council as a whole. Except for the domestic counterintelligence and counterterrorism functions of the Federal Bureau of Investigation and the Department of Homeland Security, all IC components are focused only on foreign intelligence as specified in the National Security Act of 1947 and by Executive Order 12333 of 1981.

The position of Director of National Intelligence (DNI) was created by the Intelligence Reform Act of 2004 to strengthen the management of the IC and to improve the sharing of critical intelligence information among IC components. Supporting the DNI are various interagency groups, including the National Counterterrorism Center and the National Intelligence Council, which is the senior substantive analytic body of the IC responsible for producing national intelligence estimates and other interagency analysis for national decision makers.

The IC components that contribute most directly to the effort to understand foreign military forces and to monitor arms control agreements are the following:

- The CIA provides comprehensive, all-source intelligence on national security topics; conducts counterintelligence activities overseas; and conducts special activities and other functions related to foreign intelligence as directed by the president. The CIA's three principal components are the National Clandestine Service, which collects information from human sources not obtainable through other means; the Directorate of Intelligence, which analyzes and interprets information collected from all sources; and the Directorate of Science and Technology, which applies innovative scientific, engineering, and technical solutions to intelligence collection and analytical problems.

- The Defense Intelligence Agency (DIA) provides and coordinates all-source military analysis to the Secretary of Defense; to the Chairman of the Joint Chiefs of Staff; and to force planners and war fighters worldwide. The DIA manages and integrates defense intelligence resources, both for analysis and collection.

- The National Security Agency (NSA) is the nation's cryptologic organization that coordinates, directs, and performs the exploitation of foreign signals intelligence (SIGINT) and protects U.S. and Allied information. The NSA serves the needs of both the Department of Defense and national policy makers.

- The National Geospatial-Intelligence Agency supports national policy makers and military forces by providing intelligence derived from the exploitation and analysis of imagery and geospatial information.

- The National Reconnaissance Office develops and operates space reconnaissance systems. It ensures the availability of the technology and space-borne systems needed to meet the requirements of national policy makers and military forces.

- The U.S. Army, Navy, Marine Corps, and Air Force intelligence services support military acquisition and development programs as well as ensure that critical technical intelligence is provided to the rest of the IC and to the war fighters, along with targeting information in the support of military operations.
- The Department of Energy provides the IC key technical expertise and information on foreign nuclear weapon programs and proliferation efforts, energy issues, as well as on science and technology developments.
- The Department of State's Bureau of Intelligence and Research provides the Secretary of State and the IC with analysis of global developments, drawing on all-source intelligence, diplomatic reporting, and interaction with scholars.

The remaining members of the IC have specific departmental as well as national functions:

- The Federal Bureau of Investigation is the principal investigative arm of the Department of Justice. With respect to counterintelligence, it is responsible for detecting and countering foreign intelligence activity targeted against U.S. national security interests. It also helps to counter terrorist threats to the United States.
- The Department of Homeland Security (DHS), a new member of the IC, contributes to the IC's efforts to understand and thwart terrorist threats to the homeland by fusing law enforcement and intelligence information.
- The Coast Guard, which is now part of the DHS, deals with maritime security and homeland defense.
- The Department of the Treasury collects and processes

information that may affect U.S. fiscal and monetary policies, and it covers the terrorist financing issue.

- The Drug Enforcement Administration is responsible for enforcing U.S. controlled substances laws and regulations.

Notes

1 To Verify or Not to Verify

1. Paul Nitze, "Statement on the INF Treaty and Verification before the Senate Foreign Relations Committee," January 28, 1988, p. 1. 100th Cong., 2nd sess.
2. Dick Couch, comp. and ed., *U.S. Armed Forces Nuclear, Biological and Chemical Survival Manual* (New York: Basic Books, 2003), p. 28.
3. Thomas Graham Jr. and Damien J. LaVera, *Cornerstones of Security* (Seattle: University of Washington Press, 2003), pp. 1441–43.
4. Treaty on Principles Governing the Activities of States in the Exploration and Use of Outer Space, Including the Moon and Other Celestial Bodies, 1967.
5. Treaty on the Prohibition of the Emplacement of Nuclear Weapons

and Other Weapons of Mass Destruction on the Seabed and the Ocean Floor and in the Subsoil Thereof, 1971.

6. Convention on the Prohibition of Military or Any Other Hostile Use of Environmental Modification Techniques, 1977.

7. Convention on the Prohibition of the Development, Production, and Stockpiling of Bacteriological (Biological) and Toxin Weapons and on Their Destruction, 1972.

8. Graham and LaVera, *Cornerstones*, p. 294. This passage is based on "Arms Control and Disarmament Agreements" (Washington, D.C.: U.S. GPO, 1992).

9. Ibid., p. 295.

2 Soviet Secrecy Fuels the Arms Race and Inhibits Verification

1. Richard Rhodes, *Dark Sun: The Making of the Hydrogen Bomb* (New York: Simon and Schuster, 1995).

2. Robert S Norris and William M. Arkin, "NRDC: Nuclear Notebook, Global Nuclear Stockpiles, 1945–2000," *Bulletin of the Atomic Scientists* 56, no. 2 (March/April 2000): 79.

3. Thomas Graham Jr., *Common Sense on Weapons of Mass Destruction* (Seattle: University of Washington Press, 2004), p. 170.

4. Thomas Graham Jr., *Disarmament Sketches* (Seattle: University of Washington Press, 2002), p. 125.

5. John Newhouse, *Cold Dawn* (New York: Holt, Rinehart and Winston, 1973), p. 192.

6. Rhodes, *Dark Sun*, p. 575.

7. Thomas Graham Jr. and Damien J. LaVera, *Cornerstones of Security* (Seattle: University of Washington Press, 2003), p. 822. This passage is based on "Arms Control and Disarmament Agreements" (Washington, D.C.: U.S. GPO, 1992).

8. Ibid.

9. Ibid., p. 29.

10. Ibid., pp. 29–30.

11. Ibid., p. 29.

12. Treaty Banning Nuclear Weapons Tests in the Atmosphere, in Outer Space and Under Water, 1963.

13. Treaty Between the United States of America and the Union of Soviet Socialist Republics on the Limitation of Underground Nuclear Weapon Tests, 1974 (Threshold Test Ban Treaty).

14. Treaty Between the United States of America and the Union of Soviet Socialist Republics on the Limitation of Underground Nuclear Explosions for Peaceful Purposes, 1976 (Peaceful Nuclear Explosions Treaty).

15. Protocol to the Threshold Test Ban Treaty and Protocol to the Peaceful Nuclear Explosions Treaty, 1990.

16. For a fuller account of why the CTBT has not yet and is unlikely to enter into force, see Keith A. Hansen, *Comprehensive Nuclear Test Ban Treaty* (Palo Alto, CA: Stanford University Press, 2006).

17. William Gertz, "U.S. Officials Suspect Russia Staged Nuclear Test This Year," *Washington Times*, March 7, 1996, p. 3.

18. Grigory Berdennikov, "Statement of the Permanent Representative of the Russian Federation at the Plenary Meeting of the Conference on Disarmament," March 7, 1996, p. 2.

3 U.S. Efforts to Understand Soviet Military Forces and Capabilities

1. Jeffrey Richelson, *American Espionage and the Soviet Target* (New York: Morrow and Co., 1987), p. 39.

2. Christopher Andrew, *For the President's Eyes Only* (New York: Harper-Collins, 1996), pp. 221–24.

3. Ibid., pp. 241–42.

4. Richelson, *American Espionage*, pp. 127–39.

5. Gregory Pedlow and Donald E. Welzenbach, *The CIA and the U-2 Program, 1954–1974* (Washington, D.C.: CSI, CIA, 1998), p. 10.

6. Ibid., pp. 111–12.

7. Ibid., pp. 256–57.

8. C. L. Johnson, "Development of the Lockheed SR-71 Blackbird," *Studies in Intelligence* (1982) 26 (Summer): 3–6.

9. Kevin Ruffner, ed., *Corona* (Washington, D.C.: CSI, CIA, 1995).

10. Philip Taubman, *Secret Empire* (New York: Simon and Schuster, 2003), p. 214.

11. Thomas Powers, *The Man Who Kept the Secrets* (New York: Knopf, 1979, p. 99.

12. Richelson, *American Espionage*, p. 198.

13. Taubman, *Secret Empire*, pp. 366–67.

14. Frank Oliveri, "Secret Air Force Center Monitors Worldwide Treaty Compliance," *Florida Today*, October 20, 1997.

15. Joseph Cirincione, *Deadly Arsenals* (Washington, D.C.: Carnegie Endowment for International Peace, 2002), pp. 360–61.

16. Ibid., pp. 208–9

17. Taubman, *Secret Empire*, pp. 356–57.

18. Andrew, *For the President's Eyes Only*, p. 281.

19. Gerald K. Haines and Robert E. Leggett, eds., *CIA's Analysis of the Soviet Union, 1947–1991* (Washington, D.C.: CSI, CIA, 2001), pp. 290–93.

4 Strategic Arms Control Legitimizes Space-Based Reconnaissance

1. International Institute for Strategic Studies, *The Military Balance 2005–2006* (Washington, D.C.), p. 221.

2. Howard Stoertz, "Intelligence Support to the U.S. SALT Delegation," *Studies in Intelligence* (1972) 16 (Spring): 93–94.

3. Thomas Graham Jr., *Disarmament Sketches* (Seattle: University of Washington Press, 2002), p. 45.

4. Philip Taubman, *Secret Empire* (New York: Simon and Schuster, 2003), p. 16.

5. Ibid.

6. Ibid.

7. Graham, *Disarmament Sketches*, pp. 45–56.

5 Intelligence Support to Arms Control Activities

1. Richard Helms, "Strategic Arms Limitations and Intelligence," *Studies in Intelligence* (1973), 17 (Spring): 1–7.

2. Howard Stoertz, "Intelligence Support to the U.S. SALT Delegation," *Studies in Intelligence* 16 (Spring): 99–104.

3. House Permanent Select Committee on Intelligence, *Intelligence Support to Arms Control*, Report together with Dissenting Views, 100th Cong., 1st sess., 1987, H. Rep. 100–450, pp. 11–12.

4. Ibid., p. 15.

5. Ibid., pp. 16–17.
6. Philip Taubman, *Secret Empire* (New York: Simon and Schuster, 2003), pp. 353–54.
7. Ibid., p. 351.
8. Department of Defense, *Soviet Military Power* (Washington, DC: U.S. GPO, 1988), pp. 64–65.

6 National Technical Means of Verification Takes Center Stage

1. Thomas Graham Jr., *Disarmament Sketches* (Seattle: University of Washington Press, 2002), pp. 82–83.
2. Ibid., p. 87.
3. Ibid., p. 125.
4. Ibid., p. 83.
5. Strobe Talbott, *Endgame* (New York: HarperCollins, 1979), pp. 256–59.
6. Graham, *Disarmament Sketches*, p. 88.
7. Talbott, *Endgame*, pp. 252–54.
8. Graham, *Disarmament Sketches*, p. 125.
9. In general, it is easier to verify a ban rather than a limit because under a ban any single item detected is a violation, whereas under an agreement with limits, a certain number of items are permitted. This requires that a comprehensive count be obtained to ensure the agreed-upon limits are not being exceeded. This is particularly difficult with mobile missile systems that are designed to hide from detection.
10. William Kline, "The INF Treaty," *Studies in Intelligence* 35 (1991): 58.
11. Treaty Between the United States and the Russian Federation on the Further Limitation and Reduction of Strategic Offensive Arms.
12. Deputy Director for Intelligence, CIA, "Statement for the Record on the START II Treaty for the Senate Foreign Relations Committee," 104th Cong., 1st sess., Feb. 28, 1995, p. 6.
13. Ibid., p. 1.

7 National Technical Means Goes Multilateral

1. V. V. Kuznetsov, First Deputy Minister of Foreign Affairs of the Soviet Union, speaking in a Session of the Eighteen Nation Disarmament Committee, August 14, 1962.

2. Jeffrey Richelson, *Spying on the Bomb* (New York: W.W. Norton & Co., 2000), p. 521.

3. Mohamed ElBaradei, "In Search of Security," Drell Lecture, Stanford University, November 4, 2004.

4. Keith A. Hansen, *Comprehensive Nuclear Test Ban Treaty* (Palo Alto, CA: Stanford University Press, 2006), p. 37.

8 Monitoring the Proliferation of Weapons of Mass Destruction

1. Robert Norris, "The Soviet Nuclear Archipelago," *Arms Control Today* 22, no. 1 (January/February 1992)[0]: 24.

2. Sidney Drell and James E. Goodby, *The Gravest Danger* (Stanford, CA: Hoover Institution Press, 2003), pp. 44–46.

3. George Bunn, "The Nuclear Nonproliferation Treaty," *Arms Control Today* 33 (10), December 2003, p. 8.

4. Senate Select Committee on Intelligence, "The Worldwide Threat 2004: Challenges in a Changing Global Context, Testimony of Director of Central Intelligence George J. Tenet before the Senate Select Committee on Intelligence." 108th Cong., 2nd sess., February 24, 2004, pp. 10–11.

5. George Perkovich, "India's Nuclear Weapons Debate," *Arms Control Today* 24, no. 4 (May/June 1996): 12.

6. U.S. Central Intelligence Agency, "Declassified NIE Key Judgments, Continuing Iraqi WMD Programs," October 2002, http://www.cia.gov.

7. Charles Duelfer, "Addendums to the Comprehensive Report of the Special Advisor to the DCI on Iraq's WMD and Addendum," March 2005, p. 1.

8. Senate Select Committee on Intelligence, "The Worldwide Threat 2004," p. 9.

9. ODNI News Release no. 19-06, Oct. 16, 2006, http://www.odni.gov

10. Yossi Melman, "The Israel-South Africa Nuclear Tie," *Ha'aretz*, April 21, 1997.

11. Senate Select Committee on Intelligence, *Report on Pre-War Intelligence on Iraqi WMD Programs* (SR 108–301), July 9, 2004, 108th Cong., 2nd sess.

12. In his latest book, *Spying on the Bomb*, Jeffrey Richelson has made a

significant contribution to the history of U.S. and international efforts to monitor the proliferation of nuclear weapons. In addition to explaining the origins of U.S. concern about Nazi progress toward nuclear weapons during World War II, Richelson takes the reader up to today's challenges of monitoring efforts to develop nuclear weapons and to conduct nuclear test explosions. His book provides additional details on many of the issues raised in this book.

9 Conclusion

1. Strobe Talbott, *The Master of the Game* (New York: Knopf, 1988), p. 287.
2. Gregory R. Suriano, ed., *Great American Speeches* (New York: Gramercy Books, 1993), pp. 211–13.
3. Statement by Director General Dr. Mohamed ElBaradei to the International Atomic Energy Agency General Conference, September 20, 2004.
4. Suriano, *Great American Speeches*, p. 212.
5. Christopher Andrew, *For the President's Eyes Only* (New York: Harper-Collins, 1995), p. 539.

Appendix

1. "Arms Control and Disarmament Agreements," U.S. Arms Control and Disarmament Agency (Washington, DC: U.S. GPO, 1996).
2. Jeffrey Richelson, *The Wizards of Langley* (Boulder, CO: Westview Press, 2001), pp. 276, 287.
3. Kevin Ruffner, ed., *Corona* (Washington, DC: CSI, CIA, 1995), p. xvi.
4. Thomas Gervasi, *The Myth of Soviet Military Supremacy* (New York: HarperCollins, 1987), pp. 488–94.
5. Frank Oliveri, "Secret Air Force Center Monitors Worldwide Treaty Compliance," *Florida Today*, October 20, 1997.
6. The Comprehensive Nuclear Test-Ban Treaty, 1996.

Bibliography

Andrew, Christopher. *For the President's Eyes Only: Secret Intelligence and the American Presidency from Washington to Bush.* New York: HarperCollins, 1995.

"Arms Control and Disarmament Agreements: Texts and Histories of the Negotiations." U.S. Arms Control and Disarmament Agency. Washington, DC: U.S. GPO, 1992, 1996.

Bunn, George. *Arms Control by Committee: Managing Negotiations with the Russians.* Palo Alto, CA: Stanford University Press, 1992.

———. "The Nuclear Nonproliferation Treaty: History and Current Problems." *Arms Control Today,* vol. 33, no. 10, December 2003.

Burrows, William. *Deep Black: Space Espionage and National Security.* New York: Random House, 1986.

Cirincione, Joseph. *Deadly Arsenals: Tracking Weapons of Mass Destruction.* Washington, DC: Carnegie Endowment for International Peace, 2002.

Commission on the Intelligence Capabilities of the United States Regarding Weapons of Mass Destruction. *Report to the President*. March 31, 2005.

Couch, Dick, Captain (USNR), comp. and ed. *The U.S. Armed Forces Nuclear, Biological and Chemical Survival Manual*, New York: Basic Books, 2003.

Department of Defense. *Soviet Military Power: An Assessment of the Threat 1988*. Washington, DC: U.S. GPO, 1988.

Drell, Sidney, and James E. Goodby. *The Gravest Danger: Nuclear Weapons*. Stanford, CA: Hoover Institution Press, 2003.

Duelfer, Charles. "Comprehensive Report of the Special Advisor to the DCI on Iraq's WMD and Addendum," March 2005.

ElBaradei, Mohamed. "In Search of Security: Finding an Alternative to Nuclear Deterrence." Drell Lecture, Stanford University, November 4, 2004.

———. Statement to the International Atomic Energy Agency General Conference, September 20, 2004.

"Fact Book on Intelligence." Central Intelligence Agency. Washington, DC: Office of Public Affairs, 2003.

Gates, Robert. *From the Shadows: The Ultimate Insider's Story of Five Presidents and How They Won the Cold War*. New York: Simon and Shuster, 1996.

Gervasi, Thomas. *The Myth of Soviet Military Supremacy*. New York: Harper-Collins, 1987.

Graham, Thomas Jr. *Common Sense on Weapons of Mass Destruction*. Seattle: University of Washington Press, 2004.

———. *Disarmament Sketches: Three Decades of Arms Control and International Law*. Seattle: University of Washington Press, 2002.

Graham, Thomas, Jr., and Damien J. LaVera. *Cornerstones of Security: Arms Control Treaties in the Nuclear Era*. Seattle: University of Washington Press, 2003.

Haines, Gerald K., and Robert E. Leggett, eds. *CIA's Analysis of the Soviet Union, 1947–1991*. Washington, DC: CSI, CIA, 2001.

Hansen, Keith A. *Comprehensive Nuclear Test Ban Treaty: An Insider's Perspective*. Palo Alto, CA: Stanford University Press, 2006.

Helms, Richard. "Strategic Arms Limitations and Intelligence." *Studies in Intelligence* 17 (1973): 1–7.

Johnson, C. L. "Development of the Lockheed SR-71 Blackbird." *Studies in Intelligence* 26 (1982): 3–4.

Kline, William. "The INF Treaty." *Studies in Intelligence* 35 (1991): 49–61.

Kuznetsov, V. V. Speech by the First Deputy Minister of Foreign Affairs of the

Soviet Union before a Session of the Eighteen Nation Disarmament Committee, August 14, 1962.

Lowenthal, Mark M. *Intelligence: From Secrets to Policy*. 3d ed. Washington, D.C.: CQ Press, 2005.

Matlock, Jack F., Jr. *Reagan and Gorbachev: How the Cold War Ended*. New York: Random House, 2004.

McNamara, Robert. "The Cuban Missile Crisis." *Arms Control Today*, October 2004.

Melman, Yossi. "The Israel-South Africa Nuclear Tie." *Ha'aretz*, April 21, 1997.

Miller, Jay. *Lockheed Martin's Skunk Works: The Official History*. Hong Kong: Midland Publishing, 1995.

Newhouse, John. *Cold Dawn: The Story of SALT*. New York: Holt, Rinehart and Winston, 1973.

Nitze, Paul. "Statement on the INF Treaty and Verification before the SFRC," January 28, 1988, 100th Cong., 2nd sess.

Norris, Robert. "The Soviet Nuclear Archipelago." *Arms Control Today*, January/February 1992.

Norris, Robert S., and William M. Arkin. "NRDC Nuclear Notebook, Global Nuclear Stockpiles, 1945–2000." *Bulletin of the Atomic Scientists* 56, no. 2 (March/April 2000).

Office of the Director on National Intelligence News Release no. 19–06, October 16, 2006. http://www.odni.gov

Oliveri, Frank. "Secret Air Force Center Monitors Worldwide Treaty Compliance." *Florida Today*, October 20, 1997.

Pedlow, Gregory W., and Donald E. Welzenbach. *The CIA and the U-2 Program, 1954–1974*. Washington, DC: CSI, CIA, 1998.

Perkovich, George. "India's Nuclear Weapons Debate: Unlocking the Door to the CTBT." *Arms Control Today*, May/June 1996.

Powers, Thomas. *The Man Who Kept the Secrets: Richard Helms and the CIA*. New York: Knopf, 1979.

Rhodes, Richard. *Dark Sun: The Making of the Hydrogen Bomb*. New York: Simon and Schuster, 1995.

Richelson, Jeffrey. *American Espionage and the Soviet Target*. New York: Morrow and Co., 1987.

———. "The Whole World Is Watching." *Bulletin of the Atomic Scientists*, January/February 2006, 27–35.

————. *The Wizards of Langley: Inside the CIA's Directorate of Sciences and Technology*. Boulder, CO: Westview Press, 2001.

————. *Spying on the Bomb: American Nuclear Intelligence from Nazi Germany to Iran and North Korea*. New York: W. W. Norton and Co., 2006

Ruffner, Kevin, ed. *Corona: America's First Satellite Program*. Washington, DC: CSI, CIA, 1995.

Sontag, Sherry, and Christopher Drew. *Blind Man's Bluff: The Untold Story of American Submarine Espionage*. New York: Public Affairs, 1998

Steury, Donald P., ed.. *Intentions and Capabilities: Estimates on Soviet Strategic Forces, 1950–1983*. Washington, DC: CSI, CIA, 1994.

Stoertz, Howard. "Intelligence Support to the U.S. SALT Delegation." *Studies in Intelligence* 16 (1972): 93–105.

Suriano, Gregory R., ed. *Great American Speeches*. New York: Gramercy Books, 1993.

Talbott, Strobe. *Endgame: The Inside Story of SALT II*. New York: HarperCollins, 1979.

————. *The Master of the Game: Paul Nitze and the Nuclear Peace*. New York: Knopf, 1988.

Taubman, Philip. *Secret Empire: Eisenhower, the CIA, and the Hidden Story of America's Space Espionage*. New York: Simon and Schuster, 2003.

Tsipis, Kosta, David W. Hafemeister, and Penny Janeway, eds. *Arms Control Verification: The Technologies That Make It Possible*. Washington, DC: Pergamon-Brassey's, 1986.

U.S. Central Intelligence Agency. "Declassified NIE Key Judgments, Continuing Iraqi WMD Programs," October 2002. http://www.cia.gov.

U.S. Congress, House Permanent Select Committee on Intelligence. *Intelligence Support to Arms Control*. Report together with Dissenting Views. 100th Cong., 1st sess., 1987. H. Rep. 100–450.

U.S. Congress, Senate Foreign Relations Committee. "Statement for the Record on the START II Treaty." Deputy Director for Intelligence, CIA, February 28, 1995, 104th Cong., 1st sess.

U.S. Congress, Senate Select Committee on Intelligence. *Report on Pre-War Intelligence on Iraqi WMD Programs* (SR 108–301), July 9, 2004. 108th Cong., 2nd sess.

————. *The Worldwide Threat 2004: Challenges in a Changing Global Context*,

Testimony of Director of Central Intelligence George J. Tenet before the Senate Select Committee on Intelligence. 108th Cong., 2nd sess., February 24, 2004.

von Hippel, Frank N., and Richard L. Garwin. "A Technical Analysis of North Korea's Oct. 9 Nuclear Test," *Arms Control Today,* October 19, 2006. http://www.armscontrol.org/act/2006_11/NKTestAnalysis

About the Authors

THOMAS GRAHAM JR. served for several decades as general counsel as well as acting director of the U.S. Arms Control and Disarmament Agency. In Geneva he served on the SALT II, INF, START, and Space Arms delegations and in Vienna on the CFE delegation. In Washington he was part of the policy decision-making process as well as all ratification efforts. He participated in a senior capacity in all major arms control and nonproliferation negotiations in which the United States took part from 1970 to 1997. He was President Clinton's special assistant for arms control, nonproliferation, and disarmament, with the rank of ambassador; his government work culminated in the agreement to indefinitely extend the Nuclear Non-Proliferation Treaty in 1995. Graham is chairman of the Cypress Fund for Peace and Security in Washington, D.C., and of Thorium Power, Ltd., McLean, Virginia. He has taught classes in international law and arms control at many universities. He presently teaches at the University of Washington and Stanford University. He is the author of *Disarmament Sketches* (2002) and *Common Sense on Weapons of Mass Destruction* (2004), as well as coauthor of *Cornerstones of Security* (2003).

KEITH A. HANSEN served in the course of three decades on various strategic arms control delegations (SALT II, INF, and CTBT), where he concentrated on verification issues as an expert on strategic nuclear force issues. He also supported the START I and II treaty ratification efforts in Washington, DC, in the early 1990s. He and Graham first teamed up on the SALT II delegation in the mid-1970s, and their paths continued to cross on arms control and nonproliferation efforts into the mid-1990s. Hansen, now retired from the federal government, is a consultant on global security issues and a professor of international relations. He teaches classes on arms control and national security at Stanford University, where he and Graham facilitate simulated arms control negotiations. He is the author of *The Comprehensive Nuclear Test Ban Treaty: An Insider's Perspective* (2006) and "CTBT: Forecasting the Future," *Bulletin of the Atomic Scientists* (Mar./Apr. 2005).

Index

163

Bush, George H. W., administration:
and CWC, 94; enhancing NTM
capabilities of, 79; and INF
Treaty, 79; and START I Treaty,
79; and START II Treaty, 86
Bush, George W., administration:
opposition to BWC Protocol, 95;
and Proliferation Security Initiative, 116, 129; and SORT, 88
BWC (Biological and Toxin
Weapons Convention), 11–13,
94–95, 127; absence of NTM,
130; Geneva Protocol of 1925,
8, 9; verification of, 11, 94–95

Carter, Jimmy, administration:
and SALT II Treaty ratification,
78–79; and satellite reconnaissance, 56, 75, 138; and telemetry
monitoring, 79
CD (Conference on Disarmament),
91, 128; and CTBT negotiations,
26; and FMCT negotiations, 98
Central Intelligence, directors:
G. H. W. Bush, 46; R. Gates, 46;
R. Helms, 65; J. McCone, 44
Central Intelligence Agency.
See CIA
CFE (Conventional Forces Europe)
Treaty, 93, 133
chemical weapons, 13, 100, 102,
106; used against Belgium,
Ethiopia, Iran, and Yemen, 8;
used by Egypt, Germany, Iraq,
and Italy, 8

Chemical Weapons Convention.
See CWC
China, 4, 79, 102, 103, 105, 120;
ASAT system, 125; nuclear
weapons testing, 118; opposition
to FMCT negotiation of, 98;
opposition to NTM of, 96
CIA (Central Intelligence
Agency), 31, 38, 84, 87, 142–
43; development of A-12/SR-71
reconnaissance aircraft by, 35;
development of satellite reconnaissance by, 38, 41, 137; development of U-2 reconnaissance
aircraft by, 31–32. *See also* Intelligence Community
Clinton, William Jefferson, administration: and CTBT ratification,
97; and declassification of historical imagery, 138
Comprehensive Nuclear Test Ban
Treaty. *See* CTBT
concealment, denial, and deception, 40, 113–15; by India, 44;
by Iran, 114; by Iraq, 113, 115;
by Israel, 114; by Libya, 114; by
North Korea, 111, 114; by Soviet
Union, 68, 113
Conference on Disarmament.
See CD
Conventional Forces Europe.
See CFE Treaty
CTBT (Comprehensive Nuclear
Test Ban Treaty), 23, 25–26,
42, 128, 134, 140–41; entry into

Crisis, 19, 44; and LTBT, 23, 92; and missile gap, 35

Khan, A. Q. *See* proliferation of WMD

Kosygin, Alexei, 49

Khrushchev, Nikita, 33, 34

Land, Edward. *See* aircraft reconnaissance; satellite reconnaissance

Libya, 4; concealment, denial, and deception, 114; WMD programs of, 107, 114

Limited Test Ban Treaty, 23–24, 129; absence of NTM, 130

Long-range heavy bombers, 49, 75, 87

LTBT. *See* Limited Test Ban Treaty

McNamara, Robert, 19

missile gap. *See* satellite reconnaissance; United States

National technical means of verification. *See* NTM

Nitze, Paul, 84

Nixon, Richard M., administration: and biological weapons program, 11; and nuclear test ban efforts, 20, 24–25, 97–98; and nuclear weapons stockpile, 13, 15; and nuclear weapons testing, 14, 21, 23, 24; and PNET, 24; and SALT I Treaty, 50, 120; and TTBT, 24

North Korea, 4, 103; concealment,

denial, and deception, 114; nuclear testing by, 111–12, 122; nuclear weapons program of, 92–93, 109–12; withdrawal from NPT of, 93; and Yongbyon nuclear reactor, 110–11

NPT (Nuclear Nonproliferation Treaty), 25, 92–93, 108, 120, 129; absence of NTM, 130; five nuclear-weapon states, 102, 120; indefinite extension of, 98

NTM (national technical means of verification), 51–53, 71, 88–91, 120, 129, 130; adoption in treaties by United States and Soviet Union, 53–56; and ban on telemetry encryption, 76–77; and BWC, 94, 130; and CFE, 93, 95, 133; and CTBT, 95–98, 134; and CWC, 94, 130; definition of, 51–52, 71, 76, 92, 96; and FMCT, 98; and INF Treaty, 133; international reservations regarding the use of, 95–96, 99; LTBT, 130; and non-interference and concealment, 55, 70, 77; and NPT, 130; and PNET, 132; and SALT treaties, 131, 132–33; Seabed Treaty, 131; and SORT, 134–35; and START, 133–34; and TTBT, 132. *See also* IAEA

Nuclear Nonproliferation Treaty. *See* NPT

nuclear weapons testing, 14–15, 21, 22, 26; attempts to negotiate a

Graham, Thomas, 1933–
    Spy satellites and other intelligence technologies that changed history /
Thomas Graham Jr. and Keith A. Hansen.
        p.   cm.
    Includes bibliographical references and index.
    ISBN-13: 978-0-295-98686-9 (pbk. : alk. paper)
    ISBN-10: 0-295-98686-7 (pbk. : alk. paper)
    1. Nuclear arms control.   2. Intelligence service—United States.
3. Military surveillance—United States.   4. Cold War.   5. United
States—Foreign relations—Soviet Union.   6. Soviet Union—Foreign
relations—United States.   I. Hansen, Keith A.   II. Title.
JZ5665.G73   2007
327.127304709'045—dc22   2006103046